THE HISTORY
of
CRESSWELL · ELLINGTON
LINTON · LYNEMOUTH
and
WOODHORN

L.C. LEACH

First published in 1986
Reprinted 2001
by
NEWGATE PRESS, MORPETH
at
Applebys Bookshop, 60 Newgate St,
Morpeth, Northumberland NE61 1BE

ISBN 0-9528793-2-8

Front Cover: Cresswell Hall from a painting by W. Barrons.
Back Cover: Cresswell Coat of Arms

About the Author

The Author, a retired printer, is an amateur Historian and Archaeologist. He is a Honorary Member of the Watford and S.W. Herts Archaeological Society and the Rickmansworth Historical Society.

Having spent 10 years in Ellington, Northumberland. He is now living in Essex and is a Member of the Colchester Archaeological Group.
He served on the Battleship H.M.S. Revenge in the Second World War.

References

Northumberland County History, by John Hodgson.
Northumberland, by Tomlinson.
Trade Directories - Kellys, Whites, and Bulmers.
The Morpeth Herald, 1854-1945
The Descent of the Manor of Ellington, by G.G. Baker-Cresswell, and H.H.E. Craster.
Ashington Collieries Magazine.
Documents in the Public Records Office, Military Lists, Census Returns, etc.
Ellington School Log Book.
Local Councils Minute Books.
Notes on Ellington Colliery.
Lord Runciman's autobiography "Before the Mast and After".
"The Secret Capture", by S.W. Roskill.

Acknowledgements

Viscount Runciman and Benn Bros., Publishers, for permission to use the poem "Big Tom" by James Runciman and taken from Lord Walter Runciman's autobiography, "Before the Mast and After". Captain A. J. Baker-Cresswell, D.S.O., R.N., for his advice and permission to reproduce photographs of Cresswell Hall.

Curtis Brown, agents for the late Captain S.W. Roskill, author of "The Secret Capture", published by Collins in 1959, for permission to abstract notes concerning the naval career of Captain A. J. Baker-Cresswell, D.S.O., R.N.

Major T.H. Baker-Cresswell for his completion of the family pedigree up to the present time.

Information on St. Bartholomew's Church and its vicars by the Rev. B. Skelton and Mr. P. Scott.

Many thanks to the staff of the Northumberland County Record Office for their ever willing help in my researches and also to the staff of the Morpeth Library, and the Ellington Library. Thanks also to the N.C.B. for checking my notes on Ellington Colliery and the R.N.L.I for supplying a list of shipwrecks and for permission to publish.

Members of the Mackay family were at all times willing to fetch the heavy volumes of the Morpeth Herald, which were bound in yearly editions, from 1854-1945, for my perusal.

Mr. Sampson allowed me to use his article "Shades of Trafalgar" which was published in "Northumbriana". The Editor, Mr. R. Bibby, gave permission for me to abstract it from the magazine. Mrs. D. Wharton gave me access to notes and press cuttings, also the use of photographs pertaining to the Brown family. Other information on the family was given by Mrs. Proctor. I was also able to examine the Council Minute Books for Ellington, Cresswell and Lynemouth, thanks to the respective Clerks, Mrs. Smith, Mr. J. Morris, and Mr. J. Bell. Thanks also to the Castle Morpeth Borough Council for the grant towards the cost of publication.

Many local people gave me information. Mr. W. Barrons was most helpful in allowing me to use his notes on local history. Mr. and Mrs. Wood gave me information on Hagg Farm. Mr. L. Hallowell and the Late Mr. W. Hallowell and Mr. A. Robson were very helpful in their recollections of village life.

Mr. Stan Cowton supplied many details concerning the local choral and operatic societies.

Mr. G. Sweet gave me access to his bound volumes of the Ashington Colliery Magazine, and Mr. T. Mertens provided notes on his inventions.

Mr. G. Horn had much to tell of life in Linton.

Lastly, my grateful thanks to my wife for her advice and checking the manuscript and to Mrs. J. Dawson for typing and Mr. Derek Rochester for photocopying.

CONTENTS

Foreword

The gathering together of dates and events are important because they serve as a basis upon which we can get some idea of how the people lived in bygone days.

By far the greatest effect on the lives of the ordinary people was the economic growth of a village. Of the villages covered by this history it can be seen that Cresswell and Ellington had roughly the same population in the 19th Century. However, the occupations were different. Fishing was the mainstay of Cresswell, whereas Ellington had tradesmen such as cartwrights, wheelwrights, blacksmiths and masons. Cresswell Hall was built in the 1920's and it provided work for the people of both villages and from further afield. After the Hall was built, staff was needed for its maintenance so there would have been domestic servants, gardeners, woodmen, stable hands and agricultural workers for the surrounding farms.

The two villages complemented each other in other ways. Cresswell had the church and Ellington had the vicarage. Both villages had schools, although the one at Cresswell closed towards the end of the century. The villages had two inns until near the end of the century. Today only Ellington has one.

During 1909-10 a major change took place which was to have a profound effect on both villages. This was the sinking of the first shaft for the new colliery. And with the subsequent building of the colliery rows in Ellington, the population expanded.

Cresswell's fishing industry went into a gradual decline as men forsook the sea for jobs in the pit and with the breakup of the Cresswell estate in 1924 there were less jobs for the local people.

Lynemouth now comes into the picture because in the early 1920's where there were only two farms, a mini-town was built, mainly by the Ashington Coal Company who purchased the land. In but a few years many houses were built, shops, a church, an hotel, an Institute and a school. Some of the men worked at the Ellington and Ashington collieries, as it was not until 1934 that the Lynemouth colliery was opened up.

Once again there is a change in the growth of the villages. Not very much in Cresswell but a glance at the latest population census shows that there are now more people living in Ellington than in Lynemouth. This has come about with the building of the Highthorne Estate over the last eight years.

Although some of the newcomers are miners, the majority are in other trades and professions which necessitates commuting to the surrounding towns.

Another point of interest is the fact that there are roughly the same number of shops in Lynemouth today as there were in the 1920's, although some have changed their type of business. Ellington on the other hand is now reduced to one shop. The main reason for this is that in Lynemouth a whole community came into being at a time when very few people owned cars and there were no supermarkets to entice customers to do all their shopping under one roof, although the Co-operative stores did have much the same idea with their various departments now largely phased out in the villages.

Linton had been a colliery village since 1895. It had the usual rows, school, an Institute, and a small building which served as a church and was also used for other functions. There were some shops, including a Co-operative Store.

With the closure of the pit in 1970, it became a rural village with miners having to commute to other pits or change their occupations.

The Geology of the Area

The physical landscape today presents an area of undulating land containing pasture and arable fields.

There are few woods, Chugdon and Hall Woods being the largest with just a few odd copses including the Springwell Plantation. There are two rivers, the Lyne Burn and Blakemoor Burn. Along the coast stretches the beautiful Druridge Bay, composed of grassy dunes to the north and at Cresswell a 1½ mile reef of rocks exposed at low tide has many pools in which to explore the marine life. There is a lagoon which is large enough to swim in, although caution is needed when there is a strong outgoing tide. On the beach near the dunes the sea sometimes takes away more sand than usual, revealing the blackened tree stumps and roots of a submerged forest caused by a change in the level of the sea a few thousand years ago. Also revealed at this time are modern intrusions of concrete blocks, placed there in the 1939-45 war to prevent seaborn invasion.

To the south, rocks abound, largely composed of sandstone, shales, limestone and the odd intrusion of dolerite, quartz, etc. Hereto the rocks spread inland, rising to form cliffs, stretching along the coast to Lynemouth. In the same direction there can be seen the petrified remains of another forest which existed millions of years ago. A very fine example of one of these fossilised trees was once in the conservatory of Cresswell Hall and can now be seen in the Hancock Museum, Newcastle. The tree measures 7'4" (2.235m) in girth and 5'8" (1.74m) in height. The petrified remains of plants of the euphorbia and cactus varieties are to be found in alternating stratums of schist and soft limestone. Also to be found along this stretch of the coast is the sea-coal, brought in by the tides. It varies between fine dross and small nuts. Underlying the surface features there are carboniferous coal bearing strata at varying depths. These are for the most part overburdened by boulder clay.

Near Highthorne Farm there are bands of sand under the clay, but no coal. However, there is coal to the north of the farm under clay and shale.

At one point near the coast, coal is to be found at less than two metres under sandstone, this is followed by shales and more sandstone. Elsewhere different qualities of coal are to be found at varying depths.

Coal is mined at a considerable depth under the sea and extending over six miles out.

A fault exists near Cresswell Farm. It extends out under the sea. There is another fault running nearly parallel to Cresswell Road. This also extend seawards.

Fossil plants most frequently to be found in the coal measures are Sigmaria (root), Lepidodenron (bark), Annularia, Pecopteris, Rhodea and Alethopteris (leaves). Examples of segmented reed type fossils are also to be found, such as Calamites and Cordaites.

Birds

The following birds can be seen locally:— Great Northern Diver, Red Throated Diver, Great Crested Grebe, Slavonian Grebe, Mallard, Garganey, Scaup, Long Tailed Duck, Common Scoter, Shelduck, Pink Footed Goose, Bewicks Swan, Lapwing, Little Ringed Plover, Golden Plover, Snipe, Black Tailed Godwit, Bar Tailed Godwit, Wood-Sand Piper, Redshank, Spotted Redshank, Greenshank, Little Stint, Sanderling, Ruff, Red-necked Phalarope, Common Gull, Great Spotted Woodpecker, Stonechat, Whinchat, Grasshopper Warbler, Pied Wagtail, Grey Strike, Corn Bunting, Kestrel, Mistle Thrush, Sand Martin, Goldfinch.

Birds to be seen in most gardens:— Tree Sparrow, House Sparrow, Hedge Sparrow (Dunnock), Robin, Song Thrush, Blue Tit, Coal Tit, Blackbird, Magpie, Wagtail, Chaffinch, Skylark, Yellow-Hammer, Swallow, Wood Pigeon, Wren.

Early History

There is little to show for the Prehistoric period in the area covered by this book. Some worked flints were found between Cresswell and Newbiggin by Mr. Trechmann in 1904. The finds were reported in ArchAeliana for that year.

Neolithic axes have been found at Stannington, so it is quite likely that there was some local habitation. The Bronze Age and Iron Age are not locally represented but there is ample evidence of their occupation in the mid and northern parts of the county. There are many hill forts to be found and stones with cup and ring marks. Bronze Age weapons and other artifacts from the county are to be seen in many museums.

In 1983 the erosion of the dunes between Hauxsley and Hadston revealed a large circular cairn in a pit lined with stone slabs containing a skeleton and some flint artifacts, one of which was a knife. Just behind this cairn was a smaller one containing another skeleton.

This may well have been a cemetery as further inland the area was worked for open-cast coal and there were reports of stone slabs being found.

The date of these finds is between 2000 and 1500 BC. There is a complete absence of Roman material locally. Woodhorn Church has some Saxon remains. These can be seen in the base of the tower where there are examples of "long and short work", indicative of the period. More evidence came to light in 1982 when a trial excavation near the altar revealed Saxon footings.

The fact that a church was built there suggests the possibility of a nearby settlement. However, this has not been proved by material evidence.

There is some Norman work in the church but no trace of secular building has been found locally. Part of a medieval tombstone was found when the houses in St. Bartholomew's Close, Cresswell, were built in the early 1970's. Where it came from poses a problem. One possible source is the chapel which John Hodgson states was built onto the nearby Cresswell Tower. A remote possibility is the 14th Century Preceptory of St. John of Jerusalem at Chibburn. The stone is now in the Woodhorn Museum.

There is scant evidence of early habitation in the area, but no doubt more will be found in the future.

Cresswell

Cresswell is named from a spring of fresh water at the east end of the village, where it was said water cresses grew. The village was mainly populated by fisherfolk.

During the feudal period, it was in the manor of Ellington and in the Balliol Barony. John de Balliol was Regent of Scotland and founder of Balliol College, Oxford. It was also in the parish of Woodhorn.

The following paragraph was taken from J. Hodgson's History of Northumberland and contains some words which are not in general use today:—

"The Cresswell family therefore and other proprietors in it, not holding their lands 'in capite' and the escheator consequently not making any inquisitions after their death, until the Barony fell into the hands of the crown by the attainder of the Earl of Westmorland, in the reign of Queen Elizabeth I."

The history of the Cresswell family has been made more difficult by the lack of written evidence for the early period. They do, however, appear in various private and public records as being the principal owners of land in the village.

An early manuscript states that Sir Robert de Cresswell had possession of the estate in 1191, in the reign of Richard I. Deeds respecting land in Ellington were witnessed in the reign of King John and his son Henry III by Utting or Uethred de Cresswell, Robert Bertram, Gerard of Widdrington and others.

Roger, the son of Utting de Cresswell, occurs in a pleading in 1244, as a manucaptor of Robert Cresswell who was reputed to be the father of Simon and grandfather of Roger de Cresswell. An old document states that Henry Wodryngton (Widdrington) confirms by deed in 1513 to George Cresswell his rights in lands occupied by grant from his father Rafe Wodryngton (Widdrington).

An entry for 1535 states that Margery Fenwick of Stanton entailed lands in Cresswell to her son Thomas.

In 1552, by deed poll indented grant, sale and living comprising two messuages and land to Robert Whitstone, haberdasher, of London.

In 1568 Oswald Cresswell, John Atkinson, and Cuthbert Musgrove by the Queen's feodary held land in Cresswell.

The 19th volume of records in the office of the Auditor of land revenue contains a document made in the reign of Elizabeth I in respect of lands in Cresswell and the Public Records Office have estate deeds going back to 1597.

In 1628 Robert Humphry and Nicholas Atkinson were summoned as jurors in the assizes at Newcastle.

In the same year the High Sheriff of the county was exonerated at the exchequer from the payment of £2 out of the mill of Cresswell and for the same sum charged upon the estate of John Cresswell and for £10 on that of Ephraim Widdrington in Cresswell.

In 1663 Sir Francis Radcliff, Mr. Ephraim Cresswell, Mr. William Cresswell, John Cresswell Esq., William Singleton, William Brown and widow Humphry were owners of the village.

Sir Francis Radcliff owned the north side of Cresswell, but later sold it to the Cooks of Amble New Hall, a descendent of whom of the Blakemoor line sold part of it to A.J. Baker-Cresswell who with his father Francis owned the whole of the township excepting Blakemoor. However, as previously stated earlier entries give the names of other owners.

Another source states that in 1693, Henry Singleton, yeoman of Cresswell, conveyed to George Singleton, a cottage occupied by Cuthbert Snawdon together with 8 acres of arable land and other fields named Kellyards, Kellyards Head, Havers, Flower Dykes, Morland Hill, Morland, and a further two acres of meadow riggs named Thruly Field and also pasture named Westfield, Ryehill, Long Detherish, Billish, Billish Headlands and the Side.

The Tower, which is described in a later chapter is dated to the 13th or 14th century, but the former date ties in better with the pedigree of the earliest Cresswells, because presumably they would have lived in the fortified tower.

No date is recorded for the building of a mansion and chapel which was attached to the tower, but both mansion and chapel were demolished by William Cresswell in 1749 in order to build another one on the same site.

Presumably he was then living at Woodhorn Demesne in the Red House which he had purchased from the York Building Co. in 1750. They in turn had purchased it from Lord Widdrington. The house is described as having extensive sea views and there were 303 acres of land.

An entry in Hodgson's History of Northumberland says, "and afterwards at Cresswell". However, he cannot have resided for very long in the new mansion because in 1772 it was advertised to be let, in the "Newcastle Courant". It was finally tenanted by several families of labouring people and was eventually demolished in 1845. William Cresswell left his estate in Woodhorn Demesne to be divided amongst his daughters. John Addison, the husband of Elizabeth, one of the daughters, bought the shares of her sisters in it and left it to her for life with the remainder to her nephew Francis Cresswell and his eldest son A.J. Cresswell.

There is a Red House which was built in 1927 in Woodhorn village but it has no connection with the house of that name which was in Woodhorn Demesne. No trace of the old one can be seen today. The last entry in the pedigree for a Cresswell living there is of Juliana, one of the daughters of William Cresswell. She died there in 1829 aged 92.

Referring once more to the Cresswell pedigree, it will be seen that the family descended in the male line until the death of John Cresswell in 1781. He had twin daughters but no sons. Catherine Grace was the co-heir with her sister Frances Dorothea. Frances Dorothea married Francis Easterby, an Elder Brother of Trinity House and nephew of John Addison of Woodhorn Demesne. He purchased his sister in law's moiety of Cresswell and assumed the name and arms of Cresswell in 1807.

His eldest son who was born in 1788 was named Addison John Cresswell. The name and arms of Baker were added in 1840, after his marriage to Elizabeth Mary Reed. John Baker was her cousin and on his death she inherited a considerable fortune. It was this money which enabled the new Cresswell Hall to be built in 1821, also the purchase of much of the surrounding land, together with estates further afield. Old Moor was purchased for £11,500, Hadstone and Link House for £35,000, Birdhope Craig, Woolaw, and a share of Siloans for £15,000. He also bought an estate at Bewick as well as land at New Bewick, East Lilburn and Harehope. The eldest son of this marriage was named Oswin Addison Baker-Cresswell who married Ann Seymour Conway daughter of Sir William Gordon Cumming.

Oswin Addison died in 1856. Memorials to him and to his sister Emma Elizabeth, who died in 1820, and to his brother William Gilfred, who was a captain in the XIth Hussars and died in 1854 aged 29 before the battle of Alma in the Crimea, are in the church at Cresswell.

The eldest son of Oswin Addison was born in 1844 and was named Oswin Cumming. The second son, Gilfred George was born in 1848. Oswin Addison died in 1856, within the lifetime of his father, so his son Oswin Cumming did not inherit the estate until the death of his grandfather in 1879 aged 91. Oswin Cumming married Emma Georgina Denman. He died in 1886. In 1892 his widow married the 2nd Earl of Ravensworth who died in 1903. She then married Mr. James Wadsworth in

1904 and died in 1939 aged 97 at Hove, Sussex.

The eldest son of the first marriage was Addison Francis Baker-Cresswell, born in 1874. He married Idonea, second daughter of Major Widdrington of Newton Hall. Addison Francis died in 1921 and the estate was sold in 1924. The eldest son of this marriage was John, a Lieutenant in the Royal Navy. Unfortunately he was drowned at Portsmouth when only 21 years of age.

The surviving son, Captain Addison Joe Baker-Cresswell, D.S.O., R.N., was born in London in 1901. His early years were spent at Cresswell and his career in the Royal Navy started after leaving Gresham School in Norfolk. As a Lieutenant he specialised in navigation, serving in many classes of ship from submarine to battleship.

He graduated as a Commander in the Naval Staff College and then went on a course to the R.A.F. Staff College, but because of the imminence of the war he left there in August 1939 before the completion of his course, to become a naval representative of the Middle East Planning Staff. He acted as liaison officer between General Wavell and Admiral Cunningham.

In October 1940 he accepted the command of the supply ship H.M.S. Breconshire and acted as Commodore of an important convoy bound for Malta with a cargo of much needed oil, petrol and ammunition.

After completing this operation which was escorted by the Mediterranean Fleet he joined the battleship Ramilies and took part in Admiral Sommeville's action with the Italian Fleet. He subsequently transferred to the aircraft carrier Argus, safely reaching the Clyde in December 1940. His next appointment was to command the 3rd Escort Group which consisted of three destroyers, six corvettes and three trawlers. Commander Baker-Cresswell raised his pennant as Senior Officer on the Bulldog and he lost no time in improving the efficiency of the Group.

Perhaps the most outstanding achievement in the naval career of Captain Baker-Cresswell was his capture of the German submarine U.110.

Whilst escorting a convoy in the North Atlantic a number of U-Boats carried out an attack resulting in the sinking of some merchant ships. The U.110 had sunk two of the ships but not without the Asdic operator on the corvette Aubrietia making contact and enabling two depth charge patterns to be fired. The destroyers Broadway and Bulldog had also established contact and were preparing to attack when the U.110 broke surface. Captain Baker-Cresswell on the Bulldog was on the point of giving the order to ram when men were seen coming out of the U-Boat's conning tower. As they gathered around their 4.2 inch gun he thought that they were going to open fire so he gave the order for his own men to retaliate. He then saw that the Germans were jumping into the sea and at the same time he observed that the Broadway was on a ramming course. Signalling and shouting on the loud hailer he told the captain to keep clear. Actually it had been the captain's intention to drop more depth charges to prevent the U-Boat from diving again. Unfortunately, by getting too close, his ship sustained a gash in the side caused by colliding with the U-Boat's hydroplane. Meanwhile the Aubrietia was recalled to pick up the German survivors.

The next order on the Bulldog was for an armed boat's crew to board the U-Boat. There were three objectives, the first to see whether any of the crew were onboard in case an attempt was made to scuttle her. The second was to seize any important documents and equipment. And the third to attach a towing line to take her into port.

All three objectives were achieved. No Germans were on board and the haul of documents was extensive. One was a chart showing channels leading to the German U-Boat bases. Many items of technical interest were taken, together with sextants, binoculars, etc. An engineer officer went aboard to find out whether the machinery could be started, but with no success.

Meanwhile, with the visibility deteriorating, a signal was sent to the Broadway for her to send her motor-boat which was larger and more seaworthy than the whaler which the boarding party had used. Nothing more could be done on the U-Boat so the Bulldog's 3½ inch hawser was attached to the U-Boat's towing-eye; no mean achievement in bad light and rolling seas. With the mission accomplished the motor-boat was hauled aboard the Bulldog and then began the difficult task of towing the prize to Iceland. Just after the tow got underway, a look-out reported a periscope on the starboard bow. Not wishing to be a sitting target, the Captain had no option but to slip the tow and search for the U-Boat which had also been recorded on the Bulldog's Asdic. Both the Broadway and the Aubrietia had reported Asdic contact, the latter having dropped a depth charge. The U.201 was known to have been operating in the area.

After a while an attempt was made to pick up the tow. This entailed a difficult manoeuvre to get the stern of the destroyer in line with the bows of the U-Boat. The two slightly collided but only a small dent was made in the Bulldog and the towing went ahead. Slowly they steamed towards Iceland but at a speed of only 7½ knots it would take two days before arrival.

The tow had been going satisfactorily but during the night the sea and wind started to rise and by daybreak it was so strong that it became impossible to hold the U-Boat on course. Moreover she was sinking by the stern. After a few hours, the U.110 suddenly reared up her bows and then slowly sank. The loss was a great disappointment for all concerned, but the two packing cases full of documents, charts, etc., pleased the representatives from the Admiralty who were waiting at Scapa Flow where the Bulldog had been ordered to proceed to after reporting the loss of the U-Boat. But first a call was made to Iceland in order to collect the German crew. The Commander of the U-110, Captain Lemp, did not survive. His Iron Cross which was found on the U-Boat was given to his sister by Captain Baker-Cresswell in 1958.

In recognition of his service with the 3rd Escort Group, Commander Baker-Cresswell was promoted to Captain. He was also given the D.S.O. for his part in the capture of the U.110. Awards were also given to other personnel.

The above account is a shortened version of what must have been one of the highlights of Captain Baker-Cresswell's career and it is taken from Captain S.W. Roskill's book "The Secret Capture".

After further service with the 3rd Escort Group in the North Atlantic, Captain Baker-Cresswell was transferred to the Joint Intelligence Staff at the end of 1941. He was Captain of H.M.S. Philante in 1943 and was in the East Indies Escort Force from 1944 to 1945 and he was present at the surrender of Singapore in 1945. He served with Naval Intelligence in 1948.

Retiring from the Royal Navy in 1951, he was a J.P. in 1956 and High Sheriff of Northumberland in 1962. He married Rona Eilleen, 2nd daughter of Hubert Earle Vaile of Glade Hall, Aukland, New Zealand in 1926. There is one son, Major Charles Addison Fitzherbert Baker-Cresswell, O.B.E., who served in the Territorial Army and was twice Conservative candidate for Berwick. In 1984 he was appointed a Deputy Lieutenant for Northumberland (see pedigree for issue of father and son).

Some members of the Baker-Cresswell family have lived at Preston Tower since its purchase in 1861 by Addison John Baker-Cresswell for his son Robert who died childless in 1871. There are three stained glass windows in memory of him in Ellingham Church. One was given by his father and the others by friends and neighbours. The organ was also installed to his memory.

Preston Tower passed to Addison John's two spinster daughters for life and then to his second grandson, Gilfred George, whose son Henry Gilfred succeeded him on his death in 1956.

The son of Henry Gilfred, Major Gilfred Edward Baker-Cresswell, served in the Royal Engineers in World War II and was killed in action at El Alamein in 1942. His memorial is in Ellingham Church.

He left a son and a daughter (see pedigree). His widow, Anne Sylvia, married his brother Major Thomas Henry Baker-Cresswell who served in World War II in the Royal Marines. He was on the cruiser H.M.S. Effingham and on the Prince of Wales when it took part in the sinking of the Bismark, and in 1943 he was in the landing at Salerno. He later joined H.M.S. Anson.

He was a J.P. in 1959 and a Deputy Lieutenant of the county in 1971.

They are the present occupants of Preston Tower and have two daughters (see pedigree).

The creation of the estate in 1821 with its Hall, four lodges, sawmill, kennels, stables, conservatory and other outbuildings, employed a considerable number of people, including craftsmen, many of whom were retained for the running of the estate. There would have been servants at the Hall, including cooks, dairy and laundry workers, gardeners, stable staff, gamekeepers, woodmen, blacksmiths and stonemasons.

Some lived on the estate, others in the two villages. The masons for example lived in Ellington, near the Ducket (described elsewhere).

The Home Farm provided jobs for the farm workers. Other farms were tenanted but still required farmhands. It must not be assumed that all the estates and farmworkers came from the locality. Hand hirings were held at Morpeth and Alnwick for domestic servants and farm hands and the last hiring I saw recorded was held at Alnwick in 1940. Only 30 people above military age were present owing to the demands of the war.

Notes taken from the Morpeth Herald and interviews with local people indicate a period of stability.

The Cresswell family played a large part in the welfare of the villages. The following is a typical example:— Christmas 1898. Local children were given a present and each family in the village was given a Christmas pudding, 1lb. of tea, and 2lbs. of sugar. There were other gifts for the sick and elderly.

Addison Francis Baker-Cresswell died in 1921 and in 1924 the whole estate was sold (see sale list). Cresswell Hall together with 11 acres of land was sold to the Northumberland County Council. There was a proposal to use the Hall as a mental institution and in 1930 as a High School. These plans fell through. It was said that structural faults were appearing; part of it had already been demolished when it was sold to the Ashington Coal Company. In 1932 it was occupied by Mr. Thomas Boutland, traffic manager for the coal company. He was still there in 1934. That same year a notice appeared in the Morpeth Herald for the sale of floorings and other timber. The Hall was finally completely demolished some time after 1938. Only the stable block and some arcading remain.

The site is now used as a tree nursery by the owners, the N.C.B. So another name is added to the evergrowing list of historic houses that have been demolished over the last 60 years or more. In 1935 Cresswell and the adjoining villages were put onto mains water supply. Hitherto Cresswell obtained its water supply from a spring overflowing under the wall in the field just off the Green. Two large stone slabs show the site.

In 1936 there was a proposal for the Air Ministry to have a bombing range along Druridge Bay and to take over a camp at Cresswell. However, this plan fell through

PEDIGREE OF CRESSWELL, OF CRESSWELL.

ARMS:—" Gules, on a bend sinister sable, three bull's heads argent."—(*Crabster Tables.*) But the arms of George Cresswell, of Nunkilling, in Holderness, grandson of George Cresswell, of Cresswell, as registered at the visitation of Yorkshire, in 1584, were :—" Gules three plates, each charged with a squirrel, sejant, of the field." Edmondston, for Cresswell, of Pureton, in Northamptonshire, gives :—" Azure three plates each charged with a squirrel gules, cracking a nut, or.   CREST—On a wreath, a branch of a tree barways vert, and on it a squirrel cracking a nut, or, between two sprigs of hazel fructed or. *Another Crest,*—a saracen's head proper."

[The descents below are in the same successive order as in the account of this family given in Wallis, excepting that he has three heads of the family, one after each other, of the name of John, from Oswin, in Generation IX. to William, in Generation XII., where I have been unable to obtain distinct notices of more than two. The descents from George, in Generation VII., to John, in Generation X, are proved by the pedigree entered at the College of Arms by George Cresswell, of Nunkilling, in Holderness, at the visitation of Yorkshire in 1584, for a copy of which I am indebted to C. J. Young, esq. York Herald. From a manuscript of the Cresswell pedigree said to be taken from old writings, Robert de Cresswell was in possession of the estate in the reign of Richard I. 1191.]

I.—SIR ROBERT DE CRESSWELL, knight, was father of Simon, and grandfather of Roger, as mentioned in an escheat of 21 Edw. I. 1293.—(*Woodhorn Misc. No. 25.*) He witnessed a deed respecting Whittonstall, while William Heron was sheriff of Northumberland between 1246 and 1256.—(*L.* 275.) In a trial at law, in 1249, John Baard and others against Waleran de Horton, the defendant excused his appearance on the plea of sickness, upon which Robert de Cresswell and three other knights were ordered to enquire into the truth of the plea ; but neither the defendant, nor the knights who took the view, appearing at the time appointed, the sheriff of the county had a mandate to attach them ; but to take Roger the son of Utting, and others, as sureties for Robert de Cresswell and his three associates, presenting themselves on a given day at the Stranda, in the county of Middlesex.—(*III. u.* 345.) Robert de Cresswell tested a deed of Robert de Balliol, without date, respecting Ellington (*Woodh. Misc. No. 14*) ; and was also a witness with Robert de Rue, mesne lord in Linemouth and Hurst in 1240, to a deed of Ada de Balliol, respecting twelve acres of land at Streatlam, in the county of Durham. MS. 326, fol. 152) ; and to deeds without date respecting Widdrington and Ellington.—(*Id.* 150 ; and *Woodh. Misc. No. 20.*)

II.—SIMON DE CRESSWELL was witness to a convention between Roger Bertram, of Bothal, and John Silvester, rector of Bothal, in 1261 (*III. u.* 41) ; to a deed respecting Dririggs, in the sheriffalty of Adam de Gesemouth, between 1261 and 1266 ; and to another respecting Ellington, without date.—(*Lansd.* MS. 326, fol. 151, s. ; and *Woodh. Misc. No. 21.*)

III.—ROGER DE CRESSWELL, in 21 Edw. I. was proved, upon a view, to be the son of Simon, and grandson of Robert de Cresswell, and to have entered upon the tenements they had enjoyed.—(*Woodh. Misc. No. 25.*) In Nov. 1291, he was upon a jury, at Newcastle, respecting the extent of the lands of Gilbert de Middleton (*Ing. p. m.* 19 *Edw. I. No. 19, in Tur. Lond.*) ; and, in 1292, Roger de Cresswell was one of the jurors in a trial between the corporation of Newcastle and the prior and convent of Tynemouth, respecting the port of the Tyne.—(*Brand's Newc. ii.* 561.) He witnessed the deed of Isabella de Welle, which settled Ellington upon her two daughters (*Woodh. Misc. No. 17, b.*) ; and was one of the manucaptors for Robert Bertram, as knight of the shire for Northumberland, in 1290 ; and for Henry de Dychand, in the same office, in 1296. He also witnessed deeds respecting Linton, in 1304 and 1307 (*Lansd.* MS. 326, fol. 152, 153 ; *see also Woodh. Misc. No.* 19) ; and respecting Roddam, in 1309.—(*F.* 68.)

IV.—ROBERT DE CRESSWELL occurs in a list of men at arms in Northumberland delivered into chancery in 1327 (*Cot.* MS. C. fol. 72, b.) ; was witness to a deed respecting Pendemore, near Linton, in 1333 (*Woodh. Misc. No.* 26) ; and had restitution of certain of his lands in Cresswell, in 1358.—(*III. u.* 325.)

V.—ALEXANDER DE CRESSWELL and Simon his son, tested a deed at Ellington, on the feast of the Holy Trinity, in 1376 (*Woodh. Misc. No.* 9) ; and, in the same year, Alex. de C. was a witness to a settlement of the Widdrington property.—(*Lansd.* MS. 326, fol. 151, s.) Wallis quotes authorities for his being a juror on two inquisitions after death in the time of Edward the Third ; and on one holden at Newcastle after the death of John de Strivelyn, in the second year of Richard the Second.

VI.—JOHN CRESSWELL being in captivity in Scotland, the king, Dec. 6, 1380, issued a mandate to the mayor and bailiffs of Kingston-upon-Hull, to take goods to the value of £40 out of a Scotch ship that had been lately captured at sea, and forthwith to give him that sum to assist him in procuring his redemption.—(*Rot. Scot. u.* 31.) One of the same name had a tenement in Newbigging in 1410 (*Woodh. Misc. No.* 27) ; and Wallis says he was living in the time of Henry the Fifth.

VII.—GEORGE CRESWELL, of Cresswell, was living in the time of Henry the Sixth.

VIII.—ROBERT CRESSWELL, of Creswell.	ELIZABETH, daur. of Thomas lord Lumley and Elizabeth Plantagenet, daur. of Edw. IV. by lady Elizabeth Lucy.—(*Surt. Dur. ii.* 163.)	PERCIVAL CRESSWELL, of Cresswell.	........, daur. of Hassale of Hanklow, in Cheshire.

IX.—1st wife, ...,=OSWIN CRESS-WELL, of Creswell, called Oswald in lord Wharton's order for the marches in 6 Edward VI. In 10 Eliz. 1568, he is also called Oswald Cresswell, of Cresswell.	2. JANET ERRINGTON, had one dau. Margery, wife of Mr Newton.	3. DOROTHY, daur. of sir Ralph Hedworth, of Harraton.	1. MARGARET, daur. of John Donnington, of " Escrike."	1. GEO. CRESS-WELL, of Nunkilling, in Holderness.	2. ANNE, d. of William Swinhow.	2. THOS. CRESS-WELL, married, and had 2 sons, *John & Percival.*
			1. *Ralph Cresswell*, aged 20, at the visitation of Yorkshire, in 1584.	2. John. 3. Catharine. 4. Dorothy.	3. RICHARD C. married, and had a son *Richard*, and a daur. *Anne.* 4. ELIZABETH C.=......	

X.—JOHN CRESSWELL, of Cresswell, died 29 Oct. 1598; administration to his effects 16 June, 1599.—(*Raine's Test.* 138.) Inquest after his death, taken 19 Aug. 1603, found him die possessed of one capital messuage in Cresswell, and of 200 acres of land, 100 of marsh, 60 of pasture, and a free fishery in the sea, holden of the king's manor of Bywell by the service of three parts of a knight's fee.

ELIZABETH, mentioned in the administration to her husband's effects, and seems to have re-married to Luke Errington, whose will is dated 11 Dec. 1609, describes him as of Cresswell, and gives to John Cresswell, his wife's son, his "browne fillie," to his brother John Errington £10, and mentions Elizabeth Errington his wife, and Elizabeth Errington his daughter. Widow Cresswell, of Cresswell, buried at Woodhorn, March 8, 1635.

CUTHBERT CRESSWELL, mentioned in the administration to his brother John's effects, and in the will of Luke Errington, who seems to have married his brother John's widow. According to his brother Robert's will, his wife's name was Margaret, and he had three daughters—*Margaret, Dorothy,* and *Catharine,* and a son, *Robert,* and *two other children.*—(*Raine's Test.* 340, 439.) This is probably the Cuthbert Cresswell who was appointed supervisor of coal-mines in Northumberland for queen Elisabeth.—(*Land Rev. Office Records, vol. xx. fol.* 94.) His son Robert was baptized at Woodhorn, in May, 1609.

ROBERT CRESSWELL, of Ellington, gent., by his will, dated July 20, 1610, left his body to be buried in the quire of Woodhorn church, and, besides noticing his bro. Cuthbert's family, mentions his nephew John, and two sisters.—(*Raine's Test.* 340.) Richard Fenwick was queen Elizabeth's receiver for Wylam and Ellington, and Robert Cresswell, his deputy.—

XI.—JOHN CRESSWELL, of Cresswell, esq. son and heir, aged 11 years, 7 months, and 10 days, at the time of taking the inquest after his father's death.

JOAN, wife of John Cresswell, mentioned in a writ of alias capias, Hilary term, 1628, and in other documents in the Swinburne MS. iii. 195, 237, and 250.

JANE and ISABELLA, both mentioned in the administration to their father's effects, and in the will of their uncle Robert.—(Raine's Test. 138, 340.)

XII.—1. WILLIAM CRESSWELL, of Cresswell, esq. bap. at Woodhorn July 9, 1635, had lands in Cresswell assessed to county rate in 1663, his father John and his brother Ephraim being at the same time assessed in the same schedule. He purchased an estate at Long Framlington, of Isaac Jackson, of North Shields, "chirurgeon chandler," which was conveyed to him by deed of indenture, with

LILLIS CRESSWELL had administration to the effects of her husband before 19 Sept. 1698.

2. EPHRAIM CRESSWELL, eldest son, in 1663, had lands in Cresswell assessed at £20 a year, but sold them to his brother William.—(Wallis, ii. 341.)
3. OSWALD CRESSWELL also sold his right in Cresswell, &c. to his brother William.—(Id.)
4. ......, daur. ; bap. May 17, 1626.
5. ANNE, daur. ; bap. August 5, 1628.

livery and seizin, indorsed 12 March, 1678. He died before 19 Sep. 1698, as appears by an indenture of that date between Lillis Cresswell his widow, and his sons Robert and Henry, by which, administration to his effects having been granted to his widow, on the 14th day of the same month, he made assignment of such administration to her son Robert, upon trust, to pay his father's debts, and divide the surplus between him and his brother Henry, providing that if any part of such surplus were due to Jane, daur. of the said William Cresswell, deceased, and then wife of Edward Manners, of Acton, he the said Robert, should be accountable for such part to the said Edward Manners and Jane his wife.—(Indent. penes W. Lawson de Longhurst, arm.) Wallis, whose book was printed in 1769, says that this William "was succeeded by his son Wm Cresswell, esq. father of the present possessor William Cresswell, esq. who hath one son John, and several daughters."

XIII.—WILLIAM CRESSWELL, of Cresswell, esq. son and heir. Will dated 18 May, 1749, in which his estate is described as consisting of lands at Cresswell, Bog-hall, Long Framlington, Morpeth, Potling, and Ellington. See abstract of his will among gleanings below No. 8.

ROBERT CRESSWELL, of Newcastle on Tyne, in 1698, had assignment of administration to his father's effects from his mother Lillis Cresswell. Licence to marry granted 27 August, 1700, to Robert Cresswell, of St Andrew's, Newcastle, and Anne Tully, of All Saints, wid.—(Raine's Test. 27.)

HENRY CRESSWELL, of Cresswell, in 1698. Licence to marry granted 6 Dec. 1700, to Henry Cresswell, of Newc. gt. & Jane Wilkinson, spinster.—(Raine's Test. 23.)

JANE CRESSWELL, wife of Edw. Manners, of Acton, in 1698. Licence for their marriage was granted 23 Aug. 1688.——(Raine's Test. 87.)

XIV.—WILLIAM CRESSWELL, esq. of Woodhorn Demesne in 1749, and afterwards of Cresswell, called Wm Cresswell, jun. of the Red-house, in the poll book for 1748, at which election he voted for lands in Hauxley. This is the William Cresswell who made the modern additions to the old tower of Cresswell. He left his estate of Woodhorn Demesne to be divided amongst his daughters; and John Addison, the husband of Elizabeth, bought the shares of her sisters in it, and left it to her for her life, with remainder to her nephew Francis Cresswell, and his eldest son A. J. Cresswell, esquires.

GRACE, daur. of Francis Forster, of Low Buston, died at Morpeth, 18 Aug. 1772.

XV.—JOHN CRESSWELL, of Cresswell, esq. only son and heir, in an indenture of Nov. 20, 1773, is described as inheriting from his father, lands at Cresswell, Bog-hall, Hauxley, Long Framlington, Oldmoor, Potling, and Ellington. He sold the estate at Long Framlington ; and died of a fever, in Westminster, 10 Jan. 1781.

CATHARINE da. of John Dyer, of Abberglasyn, Wales, esq.

1. CATHARINE, eldest daur. married William Johnson, of Woodhorn.
2. DOROTHY died unmarried.   3. GRACE died unmarried.
4. ELIZABETH, married at Woodhorn, June 17, 1767, to JOHN ADDISON, of Whitby and Appleton, in the county of York. She died at Woodhorn Demesne, Dec. 1, 1807, aged 68, and was buried at Woodhorn, where there is a monument in the church to her memory.—(See above, p. 186.) Mrs Addison purchased one-third part of Bewick for £16,000 ; and left it to her nephew A. J. Cresswell Baker, esq.
5. LILIA married the REV. ROBERT SANDERSON, master of the grammar school at Morpeth, and curate of Hebburn, by whom she had issue one son, who was a captain in the royal navy, and two daughters :—1. Maria, married to Sir George William Leeds, of Croxton Park, in the coun. of Cambridge, baronet ; 2. Anne, married William Burrell, of Alnwick, esq.
6. JULIANA, lived at Woodhorn Demesne, where she died October 7, 1829, aged 92.
7. BRIDGET, married at Woodhorn, 5 Nov. 1765, to HARRY PARKER, of New Norfolk Street, Grosvenor Square, London, esq. afterwards SIR H. PARKER, of Melford Hall, in the county of Suffolk, baronet, by whom she had issue—Sir William Parker, baronet, and two other sons and two daughters.
8. ALICE, wife of the REV. GEO. SMALRIDGE, rector of Bothal ; and afterwards of the REV. EDW. OTTER, rector of Bothal.

XVI.—FRANCIS DOROTHEA CRESSWELL, twin daughter and co-heir.

FRANCIS EASTERBY, of Blackheath, in the coun. of Kent, who purchased Mrs Brown's moiety of the Cresswell estate, and took the name and arms of CRESSWELL, and is now living Sept. 7, 1829, at Old Brompton, in the county of Middlesex.

CATHARINE GRACE CRESSWELL, twin sister of Mrs Cresswell, and co-heir of her father, married BIRNIE BROWN, esq. and has issue four sons—James, Birnie, Walter, & William ; and three daughters—Elizabeth Addison, Alicia, & Arminia. Eliz. A. married at Moradabad, June 5, 1827, to Robert Terranean, esq. who is in the civil service of the East India Company.—(Newc. Cour. 12 Jan. 1828.)

XVII.—ADDISON JOHN CRESSWELL, of Cresswell, esq. eldest son and heir ; high-sheriff of Northumberland in 1821 ; took the name of BAKER, in addition to his own, on his wife succeeding to the property of her cousin John Baker, esq. Mr Cresswell Baker laid the foundation stone of his magnificent mansion-house at Cresswell, June 14, 1821, and besides purchasing the whole of the township of Cresswell, excepting Blakemoor and the lands belonging to his father, has bought Old-moor for £11,500, Hadstone and Link-house for £38,000, Birdhope Craig, Woolaw, Hillock, and a share of Siloans, for £15,000.

ELIZABETH MARY REED, daur. of Gilfrid Lawson Reed, of Champion Hill, in the county of Surrey, esq., and cousin and heiress of John Baker, of Hinton on the Green, in the county of Gloucester, and of Grosvenor Street, London, esq.

2. FRANCIS CRESSWELL, of Lynn, in the county of Norfolk, esq. married RACHAEL, daur. of Wm Frye, esq. and has three sons.
3. WILLIAM CRESSWELL, esq.
4. CRESSWELL CRESSWELL, esq. a barrister of the Temple, London.
5. OSWALD JOSEPH CRESSWELL, in holy orders ; vicar of Seaham, county palatine of Durham.
6. ELIZABETH died May 2, 1827.
7. FRANCES.   8. JANE CATHARINE died Jan. 31, 1828.

XVIII.—OSWIN ADDISON, born April 10, 1819.
FRANCIS JOHN, born Feb. 20, 1822 ; died March 20, 1827.
WILLIAM GILFRID, born March 21, 1825.

ANNA FANNY, born April 9, 1827.
HENRY ROBERT, born August 22, 1829.

Cresswell Pedigree amended in 1983 by Major T. H. Baker-Cresswell

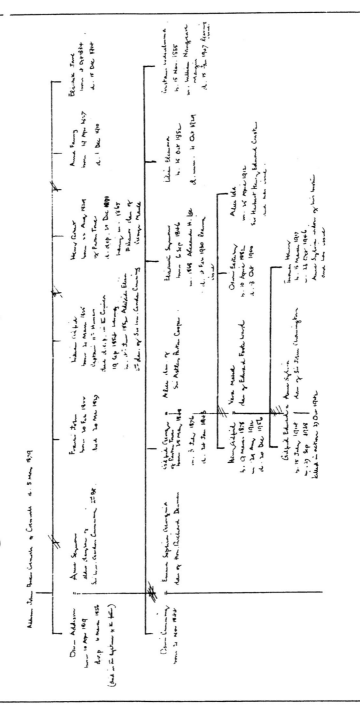

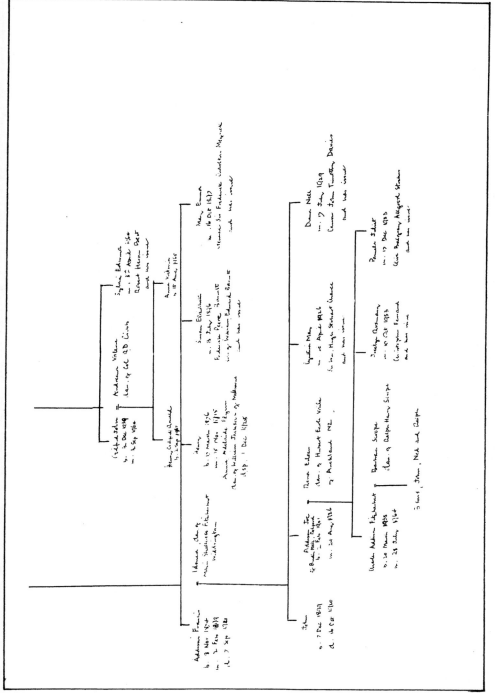

with the advent of the war. Troops were stationed at Cresswell and the huge concrete blocks which were erected to defend the shore can still be seen.

In 1938 it was proposed that a parish council be formed, but owing to the intervention of the war this did not materialise until 1948. Previously there had been informal meetings of local people. It was not until between 1954 and 1956 that street lighting came to the village.

1963 saw the establishment of the Pele Tower Caravan Site (now the Feathers). One was already in existence along the coast road towards Lynemouth.

In 1966, under the Common Registration Act, Cresswell Links was designated as a Village Green; this being a triangle of land from the church to the base of the wall on both sides of the road. Over the years very few houses had been built, but in the early 1970's a small estate near the church was built, taking its name from the church. It consists of about 14 houses. No industry exists in the village, although there is a record of a fire destroying an Eastern Motor Services garage and three vehicles. Also there was at one time a chicken farm based in the stable block of the old Hall. And a haulage contractor, G. Proudlock.

There are two shops there today, the one on the end selling icecreams, minerals, etc. was once owned by an Italian who also sold groceries. The other shop had a sub-post office, established in the 1930's, but this has been transferred to a nearby house.

Recreation and Sport

Many of the social activities of the villagers were centred around Cresswell Hall. Its garden was the venue for the annual show of the Horticultural Society which was founded between 1850 and 1852.

One of the features was a display of plants and flowers raised in the Hall conservatory, younger members of the Baker-Cresswell family competing with the local people in exhibiting flowers which they had raised. Prizes took the form of joints of meat and groceries.

A cricket team was formed in 1867 and was still flourishing in 1883. A match that Summer fielded a team composed of the following players:— G. Crozier 0, J. Creighton 1, F. Wetheral 4, Rev. Taylor 0, J. Chirney 1, H. Proctor 5, E. Fox 4, L. Finley 0, G. Alexander 11, J. Finley 0, J. Little 1.
TOTAL: 27 They lost to Waddrington.

There is no record of when the team disbanded but it is certainly many years ago.

In 1890, a branch of the Primrose League Habitation was founded and a banner was given to Mrs. Baker-Cresswell, the President. There were 153 members.

Capt. Forester contributed literature to form a reading room in Cresswell School in 1897 and there was a membership of 29. There were 20 pupils in a violin class that was formed at the church in 1906.

In January 1922, there was a notice in the "Morpeth Herald" announcing a whist drive and dance by the Cresswell Unionists in the Recreation Hall. This was no doubt the school which had long ceased to have pupils as they had been transferred to the school in Ellington.

There was a branch of the Ladies Lifeboat Guild in 1927. In 1932 there were aeroplane flights from the Cresswell Flying Field, by Capt. Hall of the North Eastern Aviation Co., at 12s/6d (62½p) a time.

A branch of the Women's Institute was formed in 1949. The Northumberland Boat Club has its boat compound along Druridge Bay.

The Military List and Posse Comitatus List.

These lists were drawn up in order to have the manpower available for riots and for invasions. The country was at war with France at that time. The number of wagons and horses were also included on some lists.

CRESSWELL MILITIA LIST 1762

G. Cook	Gentleman
John Short ⎫	
Henry Davidson ⎭	Husbandmen
John Fawcett	Officers
W. Brown ⎫	Freeholders
Matt Murrey ⎬	and
W. Turner ⎭	Husbandmen
Charles Robinson ⎫	
John Robinson ⎬	Threshers
T. Bull ⎭	
John Tate	Taylor
Adam Winlow ⎫	
G. Singleton ⎪	
W. Singleton ⎬	Husbandmen
John Gutterson ⎪	
John Telfort ⎭	
John Taylor	Schoolmaster

1762 Posse Com. List for Cresswell

John Brown	William Brown
David Johnson	John Brown
George Johnson	James Brown
John Watson	Robert Brown
James Henand	R. Armstrong
Robert Mills	W. Armstrong
W. Story	R. Armstrong
J. Thompson	J. Allison
J. Purvis	E. Bell
James Barn	W. Armstrong
M. Neal	T. McClieshan
J. Dent	W. Neal Blakemoor)
J. Mills	J. Thompson (Blakemoor)
James Mills	Thomas Davison (Blakemoor)
Henry Brown	W. Sadler (Blakemoor)
Thomas Brown	John Singleton (Constable)

Mrs. Cook, Blakemoor	3 Carts, 12 Carthorses
Stephen Pickering, Boghall	4 Carts, 12 Carthorses
Joseph Thompson, Cresswell	2 Carts, 4 Carthorses
Thomas Bell	1 Cart , 2 Carthorses
W. Hutson	1 Cart , 3 Carthorses
J. Singleton	2 Carts, 5 Carthorses
G. Fawcett	2 Carthorses

13

James Dixon, Boghall
James Easley, Boghall
Alex Brown, Boghall
R. Morton, Boghall
R. Sophley, Boghall
G. Thompson, Cresswell
Matt Robson, Cresswell
G. Ayresley, Cresswell

Cresswell Trade Directories

Parson and Whites Trade Directory – 1828
Stephen Ellringham, Vict, Flower Pot Inn
John Mills, Punch Bowl and Grocer.

Whites Directory – 1847
A. J. Baker-Cresswell
John Mills, Boat Inn (formerly Punch Bowl)
J. Forsyth, Gardener
S. Henderson, Cresswell Arms (formerly Flower Pot Inn)
J. Wilson, Schoolmistress
T. Muckle, Farm Steward
Mr. Lawson.

W. Cummins, Joiner

Hugh Kerr, Gardener

D. Gibson, Quarryman
J. Smith, Mason

Whellans Directory – 1855
Baker-Cresswell
ED. Henderson, Cresswell Arms
Hannah Leech, Schoolmistress
Thomas Muckle, Land Steward – Farm House
J. Robson, Gardener
John Smith, Stonemason
Sam Taylor, Gamekeeper, Cresswell Cottage
John Wilkinson, Woodkeeper, Cresswell Lodge

Eliz. Cook, Blakemoor House
Barbara Lawson
John Mills, Punch Bowl, beer, Boat Inn

Mary Rutledge, Shopkeeper

1858
W. Cummins, Joiner
David Gibson, Cresswell Arms, also Quarryman
Jane Murray, Schoolmistress

John Forsyth, Gardener

Otherwise same as 1855

Kellys Directory – 1887
L. Finley, Gamekeeper
J. Hill, Steward, Blakemoor Farm.

E. Fox, Head Gardener
G. Robinson, East Lodge

1897

A. F. Baker-Cresswell, Cresswell Hall
Adam Brown, Coxwain of lifeboat   Henry Brown, Fisherman
Thomas Brown, Fisherman   Thomas Geo. Crozier, Cresswell Farm
Gilbert Miller, Gamekeeper to Baker-Cresswell
G. Moore, Blakemoor House, Farmer
Anthony Oliver, Head Gardener to Cresswell House
H. Proctor, Woodman to Baker-Cresswell

1901

Renner Armstrong, Fisherman   Thomas Armstrong, Fisherman
Robert Lyle, Fisherman   Ralph Robson, Headman to Baker-
     Cresswell
Otherwise as above

1910

Cresswell Hall   Countess Ravensworth
Miss Simpson, Sea Lodge
Fishermen:—
Renner Armstrong, H. Robert, James Jurr, W. Brown – Coxwain of lifeboat, T. & G.
Crozier – Cresswell Farm
Wilfred Garfield, Head Gardener to Baker-Cresswell, also
J. Ireland, Gamekeeper   Robert Robson, head Woodman.
H. White, Boatman, Coastguard Station

1925

Capt. Sanderson, Ashington Coal Co., Principal Landowners
A. Simpson, South House
Charles Simpson, Crows Nest
R. Addison, Head Gardener to W. S. Sanderson
J. &. R. Brown, Fishermen   W. Brown, Coxwain
T. Wigfield   W. Crozier, Cresswell Farm
H. Pears, Steward, Blakemoor, Ashington Coal Co.

1929

Addison Brown, Hunter   Jas. Jurr, Fisherman
Thos. Wigfield, Coast Station   W. Keen, Cresswell Farm
W. Oliver, Market Gardener   H. Pears, Steward
G. Proudlock, Haulage Contractor

1934

A. Brown, Old School House   W. Grey, West Lodge
Joseph Holland, Crows Nest (Private House – formerly Cresswell Arms)
Ashington Coal Co., Cresswell Farm   A. Brown, Mr. Hunter
Jas. Jurr, Fisherman   T. Wigfield, Coastguard
W. Oliver, Market Gardener   F. Rutherford, Coquet View

Cresswell Hall

The photographs show an imposing mansion, and it is to John Hodgson that we are indebted for his detailed description of the architecture of the exterior and interior. The following account therefore has been abstracted from his history.

Cresswell House is from designs by Shaw, and has been built under the superintendence of Mr Green, of Newcastle. The foundation stone of this magnificent structure was laid by its proprietor, Addison John Cresswell Baker, esq., during the year of his sheriffalty, June 14, 1821, and its roof covered-in in 1825. Since which time the offices and colonnade have been completed, and the stables and conservatory are now, September, 1829, in progress. For the three fine engravings which accompany this account, I am indebted to the liberality and munificence of Mr Cresswell Baker. The first is a view of the south and west fronts, and has the old tower of Cresswell and the sea on the right, and Coquet Island in the distance on the left. Number two shows the south and east fronts, with the colonnade and the offices over it; and number three is taken from the conservatory, and has the colonnade in front, and gives a north-east prospect of part of the offices of the main body of the house. In the external character of this splendid edifice, especially in the great width of the piers, the unbroken line of entablature, and the projection of the cornice, there is a simplicity, united to a boldness and freedom, which at first sight rivet and captivate the eye, as well as produce high ideas of the fertility and graphic correctness of the mind which designed it. Its order of it, which extends from the ground to the top of the building, is nearly of an Ionic proportion; and was composed on purpose for this place, rather than copied from any particular example. The *base* which varies a little from the attic base, runs through the whole building upon a plinth four feet high. In the *entablature,* the modillions of the cornice are like those in the principal cornice within the octagon tower of Adronicus Cyrrhestes at Athens, and the cima is ornamented with the masks of lions and panthers, alternately, and the soffit or underside of the corona with coffers. Antae or angular pilasters of a simple character fortify the corners of the building. On the south, east and west fronts, the lower range of *windows,* which light the principal storey, are enriched with an architrave, frieze and cornice, which ornaments are occasionally ommited, and pilasters supporting a frieze and cornice, surmounted by a pediment, substituted in their room. The upper tier of windows to the bed-room storey have architrave and sills. The *west front* is 81½ feet, and in the centre of it has the portico, a very interesting and beautiful feature of the building, and of the kind technically called *in antis,* from the walls; the entablature over it is supported by two fluted columns, and its ceiling formed by very large stone beams with deep coffers in stone between them. Here, as well as in the south front, the capitals of the columns are similar to those in the porticos of the octagon tower mentioned before; and the principal door-way, which is beautifully carved, has the window on each side of it decorated with pilasters and a pediment, forms a great ornament to this front. The *south front,* which has a range of 9 windows, measures 107½ feet in length, and has the uniformity of its line very strikingly and pleasingly interrupted by the bow of the music room at its centre, the entablature over which is supported by two pillars similar to those of the portico, and the centre window of the wing on each side of the bow has the pilasters and pediment. The *east front,* which overlooks the sea, is 93½ feet in length: it is without columns, but its centre is strongly marked by four pilasters like the antae at the principal angles of the house; and the window on each side of this centre has the pilasters and pediment noticed in the general description of the windows. This front also derives great consequence from the *stone terrace,* 9 feet broad, which runs the whole length of it, at level of the

Cresswell Hall   *Courtesy of Captain Baker-Cresswell. D.S.O. RN.*

Cresswell Hall   *Courtesy of Captain A.J. Baker-Cresswell. D.S.O. RN.*

17

Cresswell Hall. Staircase. Entrance Hall.   *Courtesy of Captain A.J. Baker-Cresswell. D.S.O. RN.*

plinth of the house, has a parapet of pierced stone work, the figures of which are in successive similar compartments, and is joined at its north end by the colonnade, or open passage. This *colonnade* is extremely simple in its character: it forms, from the north-east angle of the house, a quadrant of 90 feet radius; fronts the south and east, and connects the terrace with the conservatory. Its entablature, the cornice of which is of great projection, is supported by a series of double square columns; and, in the north wall of it, opposite to each inter-columniation, are niches formed for the purpose of holding busts or flowering plants. The *conservatory* is 70 feet by

18

Cresswell Hall. Hall.　　　　　*Courtesy of Captain A.J. Baker-Cresswell. D.S.O. RN.*

22; and this and the colonnade are not only a useful appendage to the building by forming an extensive shelter from the north, and partially hiding the kitchen and its range of offices from a view of the lawn, but from the grounds to the south and east, have a most imposing and picturesque effect. The *kitchen and offices* annexed to it join to the north side of the main building, extend 160 feet north from it, and have secondary apartments above them. The site of the *stables* is about 160 feet from the north-west angle of the house, and forms a quadrangle — the court of which is about 100 feet square, and has one side of it ornamented with a clock tower and belfry 50 feet high. As it was thought impossible, from the exposed situation of the place, to cover the house permanently and well with the kind of flat roof usually put upon buildings in the style adopted for Cresswell, one of the slate of the ordinary pitch has been thrown over it; and the chimnies, which are conspicuous objects, and were designed to harmonize with the architecture of the rest of the house, were carried to a height which was expected would carry smoke uniformly well. The convenient arrangement of the apartments, the excellent workmanship,

19

Cresswell Hall

and the ornaments and embellishments of the *interior* parts of the house are not inferior in charcter to its external decorations. The main *entrance* to it is in the west front, and consists of the portico already described, and of a hall and *staircase,* the latter of which is a very ingenious and elaborate specimen of architecture, and forms an important feature of the house: it is 38 feet long, 24 feet wide, and 29 feet high, going the whole height of the building, and being separated from the hall by an enriched stone screen, which is glazed, and admits light from the windows of the portico. The first ascent of the stairs consists of two flights, which, meeting about half way up, unite into one, which leads to the top. The second flight is supported by a semi-circular flying arch, the underside of which is carved into coffers. Bronze candelbras are intended to be placed on the circular pedestals at the commencement of the first two flights, and casts of the celebrated Townley vase on

Drawn by T. M. Richardson   Engraved by W. Miller

CRESSWELL HOUSE.

those on each side of the bottom of the second flight. The landings round the staircase, and the cantilevers that support them, are of white stone, from the quarry at Craig-Leigh, near the city of Edinburgh, and the balustrades of these and of the second flight of stairs are of bronze and mosaic gold. The two lower flights of stairs are inclosed with a parapet, which is divided into compartments of pierced stonework. Large beams, about two feet deep, divide the ceiling into compartments, which are glazed with plate glass, and by this contrivance the stairway is lighted. Each of these glazed compartments is bordered by a running ornament delicately painted on the face of it. Three casts of the celebrated fragments of the metopes of the Parthenon at Athens are placed on each side, close below the ceiling, and above the landing; and a compartment taken from the freize within the same celebrated edifice, ornaments each end. On the right of the hall and staircase, and having a southern aspect, are the drawing-room, music room and library en suite, and communicating door-ways of Scagliola richly designed. The *music room,* which is about 29½ feet by 26 feet, is in the centre, and has a flat bow to the south. The *drawing-room* and *library* are each 34 feet by 22. The dining-room, which is 36 feet by 22, is entered from the end of the staircase, and both it and Mr Cresswell's private room, which is 22 feet square, from the east, and complete the principal apartments, all of which are 16 feet high. On the north are a back staircase, and several subordinate rooms. Warm air is conveyed from an under-ground furnace, through all the passages, the thermometer in which during the winter is seldom below 60°. One thing peculiarly deserving of remark on the subject of this house, is the manner in which it has been constructed. The walls are 3 feet 4 inches thick, and built of solid squared masses of exceedingly fine stone, brought by shipping from quarries on each side of the Wansbeck, at Ashington and Cleaswell Hill.

The Gardens

The landscaped gardens had lawns, rock gardens, flower borders and a great variety of trees and shrubs. It boasted a miniature railway and a trip could be taken to view the whale bones which were mounted on a plinth. A few pieces of bone can still be seen. Details of the whale can be read in another chapter.

The conservatory housed many exotic plants and also contained a fossil tree (sigillaria), the girth of which was 7'4" (2.235m), and it was 5'8" (1.74m) high. It came from the seabanks opposite Bogg Hall where many other examples have been found, and it is now in the Hancock Museum, Newcastle.

Cresswell Tower

Various dates have been given for the construction of the Tower. An early manuscript states that Sir Robert de Cresswell possessed an estate in Cresswell in 1191, so the tower could be dated to the 12th century, certainly no later than the 13th century.

The external measurements of the Tower are 41'3" (12.57m) by 28'9" (8.76m). The narrowest side faces the sea and has a turret at the north-east corner. There is a window at the top and bottom of this side, also a small oval aperture to the right of the bottom window, possibly for letting in extra light. There are two windows

Pele Tower. Cresswell.

OLD TOWER AND MANSION HOUSE

and a similar aperture on the south side, and the west side has a slit window. There is also a fine example of a garde-robe protruding from the top of this side. On the north side there can be seen the outline of two doorways which led into the mansion that was once attached to the Tower. The line of the roof can also be seen.

The interior consists of a barrel vaulted basement from which a spiral staircase leads to the two upper storeys, the first of which is divided into two apartments, each having a fireplace. The outlines of the two doorways which gave access to the mansion can also be seen. The floor is missing from the top storey.

The turret has a window which has on its lintel the inscription "W.L. Cresswell and William Cresswell 'brave hero'", possibly inscribed by one of the masons when erecting the mansion.

All access to the Tower has been sealed to keep out vandals.

Sale of Cresswell Estate in 1924

Grange Moor 106 acres of arable and grassland, rental £268.14.4d. Also dwelling house and farm buildings. Sold for £4,000 to Messrs. J.H. & F.A. Burn, coal owners.
Ulgham Grange Farm Residence, farm homestead, six cottages, 358 acres. Rent: £476.15.0d. Sold to tenants T. & C. Brewis for £9,000.
Ferney Beds Dwelling house, farm buildings, three cottages and gardens. 133 acres. Rent: £203.6.8d. Sold to tenants Messrs. Boutflower for £4,000.
Middlestead Farm Dwelling house, farm buildings, cottage at Lowstead. 152 acres. Rent: £155.10.0d. Sold to Mr. F. Watson of South Shields for £3,700.
Potland Farm Dwelling house, farm buildings, two-roomed cottage. 147 acres. Rent: £155. Sold to Mr. N. Craigs, Solicitor of Ashington for £3,500.
West Moor Farm Dwelling house, farm buildings, three cottages. 360 acres. Rent: £306.10.0d. Sold to Mr. F. Nicholson of Sunderland for £12,000.
Hagghouse Farm Dwelling house, four cottages. 360 acres. Rent: £333.10.0d. Sold to tenant Mrs. E. & J.F. Wood for £8,500.
High Thorne Dwelling house, farm buildings, three cottages. 356 acres. Rent: £288. Withdrawn at £8,200.
Ellington Farm House, farm buildings, three cottages. 290 acres. Rent: £278.1.2d. Withdrawn at £9,500.
Blakemoor Farm House, farm buildings, four cottages. 352 acres. Rent: £372. Withdrawn at £11,500.
Dene House Farm House, farm buildings. 132 acres. Withdrawn at £6,500.
Ellington East Moor Farm House, farm buildings, three cottages. 338 acres. Rent: £439. Withdrawn at £9,100.
Cresswell Home Farm Residences, farm buildings, six cottages. 539 acres. Rent: £523. Sold to Capt. W.S. Sanderson for £10,000.
Village of Cresswell Two Residences, 18 cottages, Pele Tower, building land, etc. 104 acres. Income: £318.17.0d. Sold to Capt. W.S. Sanderson for £8,000.
Smallholdings, houses and building land:
Ellington Mill House, farm buildings. 51 acres. Rent: £123.10.0d. Sold to Mr. Todd of Newbiggin for £3,500.
Garden House House, farm buildings. 26 acres. Withdrawn at £1,300.
Blacksmiths Shop Buildings. Rent: £17.4.0d. Withdrawn at £1,300. But this and previous lot sold to Mr. R. Mavin for £1,300.
Five Cottages and gardens. Rent: £46.16.0d. Withdrawn at £720. But later sold to Mr. T. Bell for £800.

Stone-built house-shop and business premises. Rent: £129.10.0d. Withdrawn at £1,900.

Smallholding, cottage. 1 acre of grassland. Rent: £19. Sold to tenant, Mrs. E. Hallowell for £500.

Two Cottages, gardens. Rent: £16.5.0d. Sold to tenant Mr. J. Bell for £100.

Building Site. 0.376 acres. Sold to Capt. W.S. Sanderson for £100.

Building Site. 0.710 acres. Sold to Mr. J. Bell for £100.

Plough Inn 2 acres of plantation and quarry. Rent: £170. Sold previous to sale to Capt. W.S. Sanderson for £5,000.

Ellington Bank Cottage. Withdrawn at £450.

Building Site at a plantation with three enclosures. Sold to A. Storey for £220.

Cottage, gardens. Sold to A. Storey for £400.

Smallholding, two cottages, farm buildings, 3 acres of grassland. Sold to Mr. R. Walker for £600.

Cottage, gardens. Sold to G. Crozier for £430.

Building Site. 0.347 acres. Sold to Mr. R. Walker for £80.

Building Site. 3.012 acres. Sold to A. Storey for £350.

Accommodation Land. 21 acres. Sold to Mr. W. Grey for £800.

Two Fields. 7 acres. Sold to Mr. W. Grey for £185.

Building Site, corner of Cresswell Road. 2 acres. Sold to Mr. J. Dunn for £180.

Building Site 1 acre. Sold to Capt. W.S. Sanderson for £135.

Accommodation Field, fronting new Ellington and Lynemouth Road. Approximately 4.5 acres. Sold to Mr. R. Walker for £400.

Accommodation Field with frontage as above. 10 acres. Withdrawn at £650.

As above. 3 acres. Sold previous to sale.

As above. 2 acres. Withdrawn.

As above. 1 acre. Withdrawn.

Warkworth Lane Cottage. 19 acres. Sold to Mr. W. Grey for £700.

Keepers Cottage. 44 acres. Sold to Mrs. Jes. Scott for £2,000.

Sawmill Cottage. 22 acres. Withdrawn at £1,400.

Sea Lodge Cottage, 5 acres. Sold to Capt. Sanderson for £500.

Coastguard Station. 5 acres. Sold to Capt. Sanderson for £500.

Boghall Cottage. 51 acres. Sold to Capt. Craigs of Ashington for £2,000.

Lyne Cottage. Sold to Mr. W.A. Grey Junior for £240.

Accommodation Land. Over 3 acres adjoining Widdrington Station. Sold previous to sale for £350.

Plantation Land. 6.75 acres frontage Widdrington and Ellington Road to Mr. R. Walker for £200.

Plantation Land. 7 acres frontage Widdrington and Ellington Road. Sold to Mr. Walker for £200.

Ulgham Grange villa and 51 acres. Sold to Mr. M. Herdman for £1,650.

Ulgham Grange Colliery Cottages and 5 acres. Sold to Mr. J. Batty for £400.

Cresswell Hall with 111 acres. Sold to Northumberland County Council. Sale of entire estate realised £92,415.

The Church of St. Bartholomew, Apostle and Martyr

The church was built in 1836, through the benevolence of the Baker-Cresswell family. It is of Neo-Norman design with a nave and lower chancel or sanctuary. Looking at the exterior, the bellcote will be noted, the porch has a cross on the top and

The Church of St. Bartholomew. Cresswell. *Photo: L.C. Leach.*

The church of St. Bartholomew. Cresswell. *Photo: L.C. Leach.*

above the architrave the figure of the Madonna and Child. On each side below the roof there are five corbels carved in the shape of human heads. On the chancel end of the church there are more corbel heads, nine in number, with a half one where the water pipe comes down. There are also three corbels carved with floral decoration.

One would expect to see the same number on the north side of the church but the mason must have tired of carving heads because here there are only five. There are also two floral and six blank corbels.

The Interior

The open porch leads to the church door and inside stairs give access to the organ loft. An inner door opens into the nave, the first of the stained glass windows is on the right or southside and it is of no particular merit. Further along a smaller window bears the Cresswell coat of arms, a squirrel and ears of corn. There is no inscription but it probably signifies the endowment of the church by that family. Below this window there is a small plaque placed there in 1982 in belated recognition of Margaret Armstrong, nee Brown, who had a lifetime of association with rescue from the sea, starting with her heroic effort in the rescue of men from the schooner Gustaf in 1876. On the left or northside of the nave there are two brightly coloured stained glass windows between which there is a memorial tablet with the names of local men killed in the war of 1914-18. Another smaller window is nearer to the chancel, glancing upwards on approaching the chancel the visitor will see a shield bearing the coat of arms of George IV.

On the southside of the chancel there are two windows endowed by Addison John Baker-Cresswell in memory of his eldest son Oswin Addison who died at Harehope (one of the family estates) in 1856 aged 36, and to his sister Emma Elizabeth who died in 1820. The memorial also includes the death of the third son William Gilfred who was a captain in the XIth Hussars. He died aged 29 before the battle of Alma in the Crimea.

The windows have a shield with the family crest and the above inscriptions are repeated on a marble tablet between the windows. By far the most interesting of the windows in the church are those in the east end of the chancel. The two long windows each have six medallions within vivid blue borders. They depict scenes of the life of Our Lord from the Annunciation to the Ascension, and are in white and yellow. These are by Willement, who copied them in the style circa 1200. It has been questioned as to whether they are of 1836 date or much earlier. Above these windows there is another one consisting of three circles or medallions in the same colours, the top depicting a dove.

Two long windows are in the west end of the nave, but only the top parts have stained glass. Above these there is a trefoil-shaped window which also has stained glass.

The font is also at this end of the nave.

The first redecoration of the church took place in 1911 and the latest in the early 1980's.

The Churchyard

There is a memorial to Addison Francis Baker-Cresswell and to John Baker-Cresswell who was drowned age 20 whilst serving in the Royal Navy. Two of the vicars are buried there:— the Rev. Horsfall who died in 1930 and the Rev. Taylor who was drowned at Cresswell in 1894. Many local names include the Browns, Armstrongs, Proctors, Bells, Scots, Mavins, Renners, Robsons and Taylors.

Vicars of St. Bartholomew's, Cresswell

1836-49 Edmund Goldsmith – the first vicar; later Rector of Hinton on the Green, Evesham.

1849-82 J.E. Leefe. He grew 160 varieties of willow trees.

1882-93 Robert Edward Taylor. Drowned at Cresswell on 3rd August, 1894, aged 40.

1894-1930 Thomas Horsfall. Fine singer – said to have entertained the opera singer Caruso whom he had met whilst he was training as a singer, but then decided to enter the church.

1930-42 Campbell S.B. Tause.

1942-55 Thomas G. Ridley. Later vicar of Deleval and Ellingham.

1955-61 H.R. West. Later vicar of St. Lukes, Newcastle.

1961-63 A. Beniams. Later vicar of Whittingham and St. Marys Willington, Haydon Bridge.

1964-81 James W. Dowling.

1982- Beresford Skelton.

All the vicars from T. Ridley to the present day also officiated at Lynemouth.

Mr. Briggs, a Lay Preacher, resided in the Ellington Vicarage, after the vicars moved into the one at Lynemouth, but this has now been superseded by a new one on the Highthorne Estate. It is called The Church House. Mr. Briggs held services and various meetings were held in the old Ellington Vicarage.

The Vicarage

It has been said locally that a house which was built for a member of the Baker-Cresswell family became the Vicarage, but all the evidence is against this.

Having endowed the church at Cresswell, it is reasonable to suppose that a vicarage would also have been provided as this is what happened with the Cresswell school which had a house attached for the use of the teacher, all paid for by the Baker-Cresswells. Furthermore, it is recorded in the church archives that the site on which the vicarage was built was Glebe Lane; that is land owned by the church.

Therefore, it is improbable that the Baker-Cresswell family would have had a house built on land which did not belong to them, although the surrounding land did, because in 1868 some was given by the family to enlarge the vicarage garden.

Lastly, with all the land they owned it is hardly likely that such a site would have been chosen, near what even then was a main road and with a school opposite.

The vicarage is said to have been built in the style of the church, another point against its having been a private house. The probable reason for its having been built in the village of Ellington was to form a closer link between the two villages. In 1930 the rather primitive amenities of the vicarage were improved. Electric light was installed at a cost of £65. The sum of £306, £100 of which came from local diocesan sources, was spent on a septic tank, a bathroom and plumbing.

There was no hot water, only cold supplied by hand pump. Later the Ashington Coal Company supplied piped water.

The vicarage had been empty for some years prior to its demolition in the 1970's when a close consisting of a few houses was built and named the Elms. None of the Rev. Leefe's 160 varieties of willow trees remained.

Cresswell School.

Photo: L.C. Leach.

School Teacher's Cottage. Adjoining School. Cresswell.

Photo: L.C. Leach.

Cresswell. Estate Cottages.

Photo: L.C. Leach.

Fisher Row (now South Side).

Photo: S. Dawson.

Cresswell Crowsnest on left (formerly Cresswell Arms).　　　　Photo: B. Kinghorn.

Cresswell – Places of interest

West Lodge was one of four lodges on the Estate and the nearby Rock Villa once had a bakery. Opposite is Warkworth Lane, once used by carriages from the estate as a short cut to Widdrington Station. In the small coppice on the corner of the lane there is a water pump, now collapsed into the well which once supplied the nearby residences with water.

Here is where the boundary of Ellington ends and Cresswell begins. Further along on the left there is a lane leading to Kennel or Keepers Cottage, once the abode of the gamekeeper or estate worker. It had been derelict for some years but was renovated in the 1970's. On the opposite side of the road is North View. This small cottage and Lilac Cottage near West Lodge were built from the stone taken from the much higher wall of the estate.

Further along the road on the left is Sawmill Cottage. The brick chimney and out-buildings of the sawmill are slowly becoming derelict. This would have been a busy place when the Hall existed and would have provided the timber for all purposes on the estate. A very fine view of Druridge Bay can be seen from here. On the right is the much altered North Lodge. And in the surrounding woods can be seen the stable block and the colonnade once connected to Cresswell Hall, which was demolished in the late 1930's.

On the same side a high wall encloses East Lodge which overlooks the green and the entrance to the Feathers Caravan Park. On the left is the church of St. Bartholomew, built by A.J. Baker-Cresswell in 1836. The nearby stone cottages are of interest as one of them has a stone on the front bearing a squirrel which is the emblem of the Cresswell family.

Next is a large stone building named Fenham House which was once a school, built in 1838. Note the stone globe on the top. Adjoining it is the Old School House, once the residence of the Schoolmistress.

Estate houses can be seen on the right, behind the high wall which has a gateway, now blocked up, that led to the mansion which was attached to the Tower. The adjacent field has a lower wall and at one point there are two upright stone slabs. It was here that water was piped through the wall from a spring in the field and this supplied the needs of the villagers in days gone by.

Along the seafront, there are two shops, one of which sells icecream, minerals, etc., and the other sells seaside novelties. There is also a sub post office. The St. John Ambulance Station was once the lifeboat house which was built in 1876 and was no longer needed when the service was axed in 1944.

The stone cottages further along were once called Fisher Row but have been renamed South Side. They were once the homes of fisherfolk, including the famous Brown family. One of the cottages was the Boat Inn but, like the Crows Nest, it became a private dwelling before the end of the last century. The building on the end of the row is on a grander style than the others. It was once called South House but has been renamed Manor House. A stone high up on the front wall bears the date 1648.

The small cottage along on the right was once the South Lodge of the Estate.

The next place of interest is Bog Hall Quarry, and it was from here that stone was taken to build the interior walls of Cresswell Hall. This stone was of inferior quality, so it was not used for the exterior walls.

On the headland one can see the coastguard lookout point, but it is no longer in use.

Down in the hollow between the headland and the road are some low stone-built cottages, one of which was the boyhood home of Lord Runciman. At the corner of the lane leading to these cottages is the brick built house once used by the coastguard. The stone head on the front lawn came from one of the many statues and busts which adorned the Hall in its heyday.

The "Crows Nest" at the end of Cresswell Road used to be an inn called the "Cresswell Arms", and in the garden at the rear there are jaw bones of the whale which was caught off the shore in 1822. From here, the unspoiled beauty of the sea, sand and dunes of Druridge Bay stretches out as far as the eye can see. May it always remain unspoiled.

Lord Runciman

The Runciman family originally came from Scotland and they lived in one of the small cottages which still stand near Quarry Point, Cresswell. Walter Runciman was born in 1847 and attended the school at Ellington. His father would often entertain seafaring men from Blyth and the young lad would sit spellbound listening to their adventures. Small wonder that, at the tender age of 12, he ran away to sea as a cabin boy on one of the many vessels plying from that port. He worked hard and at an early age was captain of his own ship and eventually founded the Moor Shipping Line. In 1906 he became Sir Walter Runciman, Baronet, and in 1933 he took a peerage, becoming Lord Runciman of Shoreston.

His son, Walter, was a minister to the Board of Trade from 1914 to 1916 and was raised to the peerage as a Viscount, a title higher than that of his father.

Lord Runciman used to visit his old school at Ellington once a year and would

Cottage Cresswell. The boyhood home of Lord Runciman   Photo: L.C. Leach.

give sixpence to each of the children. He would then proceed to the church at Cresswell and to the cottage where he was born. His photograph used to hang in the school, together with one of his yacht "Sunbeam" in which he used to race against his great rival Sir Thomas Lipton.

Lord Runciman died in 1937 in his 90th year.

The sister of Lord Runciman married Mr. Terry, a school master of Ellington, and their son who was born in 1865 was named Richard Runciman Terry. He became musical director of Westminster Cathedral and was knighted in 1922. He composed five masses and also rescued many old Northumberland sea shanties that would have otherwise been forgotten. Lord Runciman's brother James was a poet and ballad writer. His poem, "Big Tom", is reproduced here and is taken from Lord Runciman's autobiography, "Before the Mast and After".

Victim of the "Press Gang"

In the early 19th Century there was a family of fisherfolk named McCleishan, sometimes spelled McCleish, living in the village of Cresswell. This was the time when the British were at war with the French, so the Royal Navy was patrolling the coast.

Life on the old wooden ships was very grim. The food was very poor and floggings were ordered for the slightest misdemeanour. Thus recruits were hard to find and the Admiralty initiated a body of men known as the "Press Gang". It consisted of a few officers and men who frequented seaports looking for locals, especially fishermen. They would be forcibly carried off for service in the Navy. One such unfortunate was young Tom McCleishan. How long before the Battle of Trafalgar Tom's abduction took place is not known, but on that day, the 21st October, 1805, he was with the fleet, going into battle. The name of the ship on which he served is not recorded.

Nelson's plan to break up the French and Spanish fleets had succeeded and the British ships were pursuing the individual ships of the scattered enemy fleet. A dismasted ship was near Tom's ship so an order was given for a boarding party including Tom to man the cutter. Pulling alongside, the sailors, armed with cutlasses, climbed up the side of the vessel to be met by the enemy who were armed with pikes and axes. A fierce fight ensued in which some of the British tars got on board but others were struck down and fell into the sea. Tom, somewhat dazed by the hours of battle, was the last to leave the cutter. Clambering to the top, he was just going to heave himself over the gunwale when a Frenchman looking over the side swung his axe at him. Tom grabbed the axe with one hand and at the same time slashed out with his cutlass held in the other hand. This led to disaster as he was precariously balanced on the side of the ship and he toppled backwards down into the cutter, striking his head on a seat. He lay unconscious as the boat drifted away, and after some time Tom regained consciousness. Seeing land ahead, he mustered enough strength to pull to the shore. It was unfortunately the coast of France that he had reached. The tale does not tell of how he fared, but some months later he arrived back in the village of Cresswell with the axe as a trophy. Resuming life with his father in their occupation of fishermen, he never thought for one moment that he would be classed as a deserter. However, one day, from information given by an informer, a naval patrol arrived and took poor Tom off to Portsmouth for a court martial. Desertion from the Navy was classed as a very serious offence, and the usual penalty was to be hung at the yardarm. Tom's story must have met with some sympathy by the court, as he escaped this penalty but was ordered to be "flogged through the fleet". This could have had an equally disastrous result as not less than five ships was the usual number required for the punishment. Tom's luck was in, as most of the ships were out on patrol. So, although he was flogged, he survived to return to his native village and lived to a ripe old age.

Mr. Sampson's grandmother was born in 1859 and lived in nearby Newbiggin. She would tell of when she was a little girl, the local lads used to walk along the coast to Cresswell to see Old Tom McCleishan's back, scarred with the lashings of the cat o' nine tails. One of the four jugs in the family has the name of Tom McCleishan glazed on the side. Also surviving is a piece of his cue or naval pigtail. Unfortunately, the Frenchman's axe has been lost.

This information was taken from Mr. W. Sampson's account in "Northumbriana" Magazine.

The Brown Family

No history of Cresswell would be complete without mention of this family of fisherfolk who never failed to help in the rescue of those in peril on the sea.

The family can be traced back to at least the 17th century and the Militia List of 1762 has seven men of that name. The following is a tribute, not only to the Browns, but to other fishermen including the Armstrongs, Lyle, Jefferson and Taylor.

In the winter of 1862 a foreign brig, The Julius of Alberg, ran onto a ledge of rocks partly submerged by the incoming tide. The fisherfolk, seeing the danger, wondered what could be done to rescue the stricken crew. One of the onlookers, a tall man, called out to his four sons and they all went along the beach to where the largest coble lay. The squire's cartman, who was passing, pulled up to see whether he could be of any assistance. He readily unharnessed his horse and with ropes attached to the boat, the horse pulled it to the water's edge. Unfortunately, when nearing the waves, the horse took fright and lashed out at the boat, splintering some of her timbers. The tall man, known as Big Tom Brown, immediately took off his jacket and stuffed it into the hole and told his youngest son to sit on it. Later the lad was relieved by a volunteer named Tom McLeish whose sister, concerned about the safety of the crew of the coble, screamed "Oh, dear me, they'll aal be drooned, so whe'll eat the side of bacon?". The coble pulled to a position alongside the wrecked vessel and, seeing a big comber come roaring in, Big Tom shouted to the crew of the vessel to jump when the swell took his boat almost level with the deck of the stricken vessel. Two of the seamen jumped at the wrong time and suffered broken legs. The coble only just pulled away in time as another big wave smashed the brig to pieces, the masts falling outwards and just missing the coble. Gaining the shore with all the seamen saved there was congratulations from the onlookers. There was also a jocular remark to old Elsie, Tom McLeish's sister, who kept house for him and who had been returned to her "to eat the flech of bacon noo".

This account is taken from the autobiography of Lord Runciman who, with other members of his family, witnessed the rescue. His brother James wrote a poem relating the epic rescue, and the part played by "Big" Tom Brown.

On a calm morning in March 1874 a coble put to sea, its crew consisting of James Brown and his sons, Thomas 38 years old, John 23 years and George 14 years. A sudden gale capsized the boat, and a rescue attempt by James' brother and other men was to no avail and all were drowned. Thomas left a widow and three children, two of whom were twins. The men were buried in Woodhorn churchyard. The authorities were blamed for the tragedy because it was felt that a barometer on the sea front would have foretold the coming storm.

In January 1876, the steamer Gustaf sailing from Gothenburg to the Tyne with a cargo and 14 passengers, including three women, was in distress off the coast. The local people turned out to launch the new lifeboat named Old Potter which had been given by Mr. Baker-Cresswell the previous year together with a new boathouse. Men, women and horses dragged the lifeboat a mile across the sand to a suitable launching place. Meanwhile the Gustaf struck the rocks and one of its boats was smashed, and the other overturned on a rock with four men clinging to the keel. Four times the women formed a living chain with Margaret Brown, who was completely out of her depth, at the end of the chain. Sometimes the women were swept off their feet. Nevertheless, the stranded sailors were eventually brought ashore. After several attempts to reach the wreck, Coxswain Brown decided to give his exhausted men a rest and send for a rocket apparatus. He called for volunteers from the women to take the message to the coastguard at Newbiggin. Margaret Brown and two other girls, Mary Brown and Isabella Armstrong, stepped forward, although still exhausted from their previous efforts. Margaret was put in charge. The girls took off their shoes and stockings and commenced the long journey along the coast. Two miles along, the track led over a planked bridge across the River Lyne. Parts of the bridge at each end had been swept away by the flood waters. Margaret's first attempt to reach the bridge failed, the force of the current carrying her some distance past the near end. Struggling ashore she again waded into the river, this time some distance higher up the river. Again the current swept her seawards, but she managed to clutch at a plank and drag herself onto it. Crossing the remains of the bridge on her hands and knees, she dropped into the water and struggled to safety. The other girls followed her. Hugging the shelter of the cliff, the exhausted girls made their way along the coast. In gale force winds and nearly being swept into the sea, with bleeding feet and torn clothes, they at last reached the outskirts of Newbiggin. Mary and Isabella were too exhausted to continue so went into a nearby house. Margaret continued, collapsing at the coastguard station. Rocket equipment was despatched by horse, but ironically it

Margaret Armstrong.   *Photo: Courtesy of D. Wharton.*

was not needed as the lifeboat had managed to reach the wreck and save the women and seven men.

This account was written by Mr. H.S. Hunter, a former honorary secretary of the Cresswell branch of the R.N.L.I., and was found in the archives of the institution.

The courage of these fishergirls so impressed the coastguard that they gave Mary and Isabella inscribed brooches and presented Margaret with a silver teapot inscribed with a tribute from Capt. Hickly, R.N., the Commanders, and Lieutenants of the division in the Hull Coastguard District. They were also presented with special awards by the Institution.

Margaret Brown married and took the name of Armstrong, and at over 70 years of age she was still one of the leading helpers attached to the lifeboat, never missing a quarterly practice or service launching in her life. She died at the age of 79 years, and is buried in Cresswell Churchyard with other members of the Brown family, including her own son who was drowned.

Later in the same year of 1876 Kitty Brown added her name to the saga of the family. A coble was in difficulties trying to make the shore. In mountainous seas,

Lifeboat crew, all members of the Brown Family.   Photo: *Courtesy of A. Brown.*

Kitty launched a small boat and rowed single handed to the three men in the coble. She was exhausted but they all managed to get safely ashore.

In March 1888, a severe storm along the coast stressed the need for a rocket apparatus, as in certain tides and winds it was impossible to launch the lifeboat, as had been the case in 1876 with the wreck of the Gustaf and the epic struggle of the girls in their efforts to reach Newbiggin for such apparatus.

In December 1888, a bad storm caught the fishing boats at sea. The women launched the lifeboat but there were only six men and one boy to form a crew. The usual crew was eleven men but they were all in the fishing boats. Owing to very heavy seas the lifeboat had to return to shore, but eventually the fishing fleet managed to get in at Hauxley.

In 1889 a new lifeboat named Ellen and Eliza replaced the Old Potter which had saved 14 lives. The crew consisted of: Tom Brown-Cox, Henry Brown, Henry Taylor, Tom Brown, Thos. Brown, Adam Brown, Henry Brown, John Jefferson, H. Brown, Robert Brown, R. Taylor and Jas. Armstrong.

These names were taken from the Morpeth Herald, and probably included stand-by men, as the usual crew was 11 men, as previously stated.

In March 1890, Mr. T. Brown, known as "Big Tom", received a service clasp and a framed testimonial, plus £15 and a naval telescope for having been in charge of the lifeboat for 15 years. In August 1905, three Newbiggin men were in difficulties off the coast. Two were saved by James Brown Snr. James Brown Jnr, and Adam Brown. They were all out fishing at night. Adam Brown died in November 1911. He had been in poor health for the last two years of his life. He had been a member of the lifeboat crew for 33 years and coxswain for 15 years, during which time he and other fishermen had saved 105 lives. At the age of 19 he heard his mother say that a Newbiggin coble was in distress, so he ran the four miles from Cresswell and joined the lifeboat crew. On another occasion when the schooner Forest was driven ashore he and four others took out a boat and saved seven lives. In 1881, when Adam Brown was 25 years old, the Norwegian brig Ida was stranded on Carr Rocks. It was impossible for the lifeboat to get to the wreck so Adam helped by his two brothers and with a rope tied around his waist managed to get out to the vessel. He hauled himself on board and the first man he took on his back had a broken leg. Having safety reached the shore with this man he returned to save three more men, but the last one who was very heavy was only saved with some difficulty as a huge wave dashed them against the rocks. Adam's hands were badly gashed, but nevertheless he went out again, this time to rescue the captain and another seaman but unfortunately they had been swept overboard.

On another occasion, Adam and two companions rescued a Miss Fox and her friend.

Yet again, when the vessel J.T. Mole ran ashore he helped with the rescue of the crew.

In 1921 Mr. H. Brown died. He had been a coxswain of the lifeboat and a manager of the school at Ellington.

In 1922 a gold brooch and Record of Thanks was presented to Margaret Brown (Armstrong) by Sir Godfrey Baring on behalf of the R.N.L.I. The award was for 50 years as a launcher of the lifeboat. A Tyneside man was drowned in 1931. Coxswain Addison Brown assembled a crew to man a coble but did not find the body. In 1931, at the age of 78, James (King) Brown died. He was the last of a family of 14. He had been given the name "King" by T. Terry, schoolmaster of Ellington. His nephew

Courtesy of M. Elliott.

Lifeboat, Old Potter 1875-1889. *Courtesy of W. Barrons.*

Lifeboat, Ella and Eliza 1889-1909. *Photo: Courtesy of D. Wharton.*

Lifeboat, Martha 1909-1944.   *Courtesy of A. Brown.*

became coxswain and the crew were all Brown's except for two – Sam Brown, aged 18, fell from a boat and was drowned in 1932. He was unable to swim and a report in the local paper on the inquest quotes a question by the Coroner as to why so many of the fisherfolk could not swim.

By the 1930's the Cresswell families had ceased to get their livelihood from the sea. Some had taken jobs in coal mines and other occupations. The lifeboat was still manned from local families but the calls were not so frequent, and in 1944 the service was ended. The last call for help was in 1941 when the S.S. Empire Breeze was in difficulties off the coast.

Just before the completion of this history, the sea claimed one more victim of this family. On June 3rd, 1984, 62 year old John Brown was out in a coble with a friend when it was overturned by rough seas and only his partner survived. So ends the saga of the Brown family.

Shipwrecks

The following notes are of wrecks which took place before the introduction of the lifeboat service in 1875. There are also reports taken from the Morpeth Herald of a number of wrecks which occurred whilst the lifeboat service was in operation.

1636 Proceedings in a trial of law in the court of exchequer upon a writ respecting a wreck at Cresswell.

This was taken from Martins Index.

1732 Prosecutions following a wreck (see Quarter Session Notes).

1792 A French privateer fired on the Newcastle ship Content. Invasion was feared but the Content beat off its assailants.

1799 A very bad storm caused the destruction of over 30 ships, one of which was carrying the coffin of Lady Dundonald. The coffin was washed up on the shore intact. Thereafter, the catastrophy was referred to as Lady Dundonald's storm.

1862 A full account of this rescue is given in the notes on the Brown family.

1881 See notes on the Brown family, regarding the death of Adam Brown and the wreck of the Ida.

There are two other vessels mentioned which are not in the R.N.L.I. list. They are the schooners Forest and J.T. Mole.

1907 The Norwegian sailing ship Hermanos was stranded on the shore. Local fishermen were to receive £400 salvage money for refloating her but were unable to do so as the vessel was stuck too firmly into the sand. Tugs had to be called in, so the fishermen only received £100; the rest going to the tugmen.

1920 An issue of the Morpeth Herald contains the following account:— The four-masted auxiliary schooner Adrian Baden from Dunkirk was stranded on the rocks. The lifeboat Martha was launched by the fisherfolk wives and managed to get alongside the vessel. But the men were exhausted by their efforts, so they rested on board for a while. By their knowledge of the seabed the local men were able to indicate the best position to drop the ship's anchor. The engines were then revved up and the ship was hauled free. A tug then towed her to Blyth, her original destination. Later in the year, the coxswain of the lifeboat claimed salvage money and was awarded £360. The French skipper denied that they were aground although previously saying that they were.

In October, 1920. The Steam trawler C.S.D. of North Shields was in distress in foggy weather. The lifeboat went out but, owing to heavy seas, was unable to get alongside. Lifelines were thrown aboard and the crew were rescued. After staying the night in the fishermen's cottages, the crew were able to refloat their vessel.

January 1922. The Wendla, proceeding from Norway to Blyth, was wrecked in very stormy weather, but the crew were rescued. As the local roads were blocked by snow, the crew had to spend the night in the coastguard station.

Royal National Lifeboat Institution

List of service calls by the Cresswell Lifeboats

Date	Position of casualty	Casualty	Assessment
		The "OLD POTTER" lifeboat	
1876			
Jan 5	**Druridge Bay**	S.S. "GUSTAF" of Gothenburg	Rescued 14
1880			
Feb 15	Quarry Point	Brig. "FRITHIOF" of Hoganas	Service declined
Oct 20	Druridge Bay	"DAUNTLESS" of Bristol	Took lifeboat along coast
1881			
Oct 21	Broad Scar Rock	Brig. "IDA" of Frederickstadt	Could not reach vessel

Date	Position of casualty	Casualty	Assessment
1882			
Jan 14	Off Cresswell	Brig. "SWIFT" of Krageroe	Rescued 8 and saved vessel
Dec 3	Chibburn Burn	S.S. "AMULET"	Services not required
1883			
Jan 1	Druridge Bay	S.S. "CONGO" of Cardiff	Rendered assistance
1886			
Dec 21	Off Cresswell	Schooner "SWIFT" of Laurivig	Rescued 11
1888			
Nov 27	Near Cresswell	Fishing boats	No service

The "ELLEN AND ELIZA" lifeboat

Date	Position of casualty	Casualty	Assessment
1889			
Dec 24	Headgate Rock	S.S. "CEDRIC" of Newcastle-on-Tyne	Rendered assistance
1891			
Oct 21	Chibburnmoth	Lugger "ARTEMIS"	No service
1894			
Jan 11	Snab Point	Barque "AGERÖEN"	Rescued 10
1895			
Feb 6	Off Cresswell	Fishing boats	No service
1897			
March 13	Quarry Point	Brig. "VAAREN" of Tredestrand	Rescued 4
Oct 5	Rocks near Lyne Burn	Schooner "JULIE HIDE" of Riga	Stood by vessel
1898			
Apr 30	Brig Head	S.S. "STRATHCARRON" of Glasgow	Rescued 27
Nov 12	Chibburnmouth	S.S. "BANKCHEF FASTING" of Christiansund	Remained by vessel
1899			
Feb 6	Broad Scar Rock	Steam trawler "LAPSPRING"	Stood by vessel
Apr 13	Broad Scar Rock	S.S. "NERO"	No service
Oct 17	Limpet Rocks	S.S. trawler "WELSH PRINCE" of North Shields	Stood by vessel
Dec 12	Brig Head Rocks	A steamer	No service
Dec 30	S. of Snab Point	S.S. "WASHINGTON"	No service
1900			
Aug 15	Headagee Rocks	French fishing lugger "ARAGO"	Landed ten
Aug 20	2 miles S. of Cresswell	S.S. "VANADIS"	No service
1901			
Jan 14	2 miles S. of station	Steam trawler "VALENTIA" of South Shields	No service
1902			
Feb 16	Quarry Point	S.S. "MINERVA" of Sunderland	Rendered assistance

Date	Position of casualty	Casualty	Assessment
1904			
Feb 6	1 mile S. of station	Unknown	Crew assembled
Dec 18	½ mile S. of Quarry Point	Unknown steamer	No service
1907			
Feb 8-9	2 miles N. of station	Ship "HERMANOS" of Lillesaud	Assisted to save
1909			
Jan 8	Off Cresswell	A fishing boat of Newbiggin	Crew assembled
Feb 18	¼ mile S. of Coastguard Station	S.S. "HELSUIGBORG"	Assisted to save

The "MARTHA" lifeboat

Date	Position of casualty	Casualty	Assessment
Sept 23	S. of Cresswell	Unknown	No service
Dec 22-23	Boghall Rocks	S.S. "KOREA" of St. Petersburg	Stood by vessel
1910			
Apr 17	1 mile N. of Cresswell	S.S. "CAP SPARTEL" of Antwerp	No service
Nov 27	S. of Quarry Point	Unknown	No service
1911			
Nov 30	Snab Point	Steam trawler "UPTON CASTLE" of North Shields	Rendered assistance
1912			
Jan 19	Druridge Bay	S.S. "ADELINE HUGO STIMER"	Crew assembled
July 23	The Northern Hole	Coble "THE FOUR BROTHERS"	Rescued 3 and saved boat
1914			
Feb 22	1½ miles S. of Cresswell at Keypoint	Ship "ARCTIC STREAM" of Glasgow	Rescued 6
1915			
Mar 13	6 miles S.E. of station	S.S. "INVERGYLE" of Glasgow	No service
1920			
Mar 29	Druridge Bay	H.M. Motor Schooner "ADRIEN BADIN" of Marseilles	Rendered assistance
Oct 23	2 miles N. of Cresswell	Steam trawler "C.S.D." of North Shields	Rescued 8
Nov 23	1 mile S. of Cresswell	Trawler "CASSANDRA" of Hull	Stoodby vessel
1921			
Nov 30	¼ mile E. of lifeboat house	S.S. "RARN" of Bergen	Saved vessel

Date	Position of casualty	Casualty	Assessment
1922			
Jan 15	1 mile S. of station	S.S. "WENDLA" of Hangesund	Assisted vessel
1923			
Apr 12	Druridge Bay	S.S. "KAMFJORD" of Christiania	Assisted vessel
Nov 26	2 miles S. of station	Steam trawler "GLENSTAR" of North Shields	Saved vessel
1924			
Jan 6	Druridge Bay	S.S. "BROMMA" of Christiania	Stood by vessel
Sept 7	2¼ miles S. of station	S.S. "AYDON" of Newcastle	No service
1928			
Feb 20	East of station	S.S. "MARTA" of Hambourg	Stood by vessel
Oct 6	2¾ miles N. of station	Steam trawler "DARWIN" of Fleetwood	Rendered assistance
Nov 20	1 mile S. of station	Steam trawler "TYNEMOUTH CASTLE" of N. Shields	Landed nine
1929			
Mar 18	1½ miles S. of station	Unknown vessel	No service
Nov 11	5 miles N.E. of station	Fishing coble "RENOWN" of Houseley	Crew assembled
1935			
May 28	Broad Scar	Trawler "BOSCOBEL" of Aberdeen	Stood by vessel
1936			
Jan 1	Carr Rocks	S.S. "BONDICAR"	No service
1940			
Feb 3	1½ miles N.E. of station	German aircraft	No service
Mar 29	¾ mile E. of station	German aircraft	No service
1941			
Mar 13	2½ miles S.E. of station	Tug "BULLGER" of Leith	Landed twelve
Mar 14	2½ miles S.E. of station	S.S. "EMPIRE BREEZE" of Sunderland	Stood by vessel
Mar 15	2½ miles N.E. of station	S.S. "EMPIRE BREEZE" of Sunderland	Gave help
1944	STATION CLOSED		

In 1973 the late Councillor Michael Bell initiated an Inshore Rescue Service. Fund raising projects and a donation of £100 from Castle Morpeth Borough Council enabled a boat and equipment to be purchased. Unfortunately, lack of volunteers caused the service to be abandoned in 1976, and the funds were given to the Boulmer Rescue Service.

(I am indebted to Mr. Williamson, one of the officials of the Service, for this information.)

Whale

In 1822, a large whale was wounded by being thrown against the rocks between Cresswell and Lynemouth. Local fishermen, reinforced by labourers working on the erection of Cresswell Hall, tried to kill it and bring it ashore. This was eventually accomplished by the use of a harpoon made by the estate blacksmith. The whale measured 61ft. (18.91m) in length and 37ft. (11.285m) in circumference. It produced 9 tons of flesh and 158 gallons of oil. It was claimed by Mr. Baker-Cresswell and Mr. R. Atkinson who both had property in the area. But the Admiralty stepped in and claimed it for the Crown.

Some of the jaw bone and other parts were erected on a concrete plinth in the grounds of the Hall but very little can be seen today. It formed one of the attractions for the passengers on the miniature railway which used to run through the grounds.

Another part of the jaw bone can still be seen to the rear of the "Crows Nest" adjacent to the road.

In 1889, a 13ft. (3.96m) porpoise was stranded on the beach, and in more recent times, 1944, a killer whale (orcinus area) measuring 24ft. (7.32m) came ashore. There have not been any more whales since then, only a porpoise and a grey seal in 1964.

1750 A large whale was found dead in the sea and was towed ashore.

1763 An angel fish was found alive. It measured 4½ ft. (1.37m).

Blakemoor

Blakemoor is situated on a low damp plain towards Hemscott Hill. It may have taken its name from the dark heathery moor that once existed. The 19th century farm-house stood near the farm cottages. Two stone pillars of what was once the gateway leading to the house and a small section of one of its walls still survive.

This later house was built on the site of an earlier one erected in 1663 which belonged to Sir Francis Radcliff. It was later purchased by Edward Cook of Amble New Hall, who in his will dated 1691 left all his "messuages, lands, tenements, coneywarrens, fishing and other heriditments whatsoever in Cresswell" to his second son Edward, from whom with the exception of the part sold to Mr. Baker-Cresswell, they descended to Mrs. Cook. Edward Cook had eight sons and estates at Amble, Togston, Newton-on-the-Moor, Brainshaugh and Blakemoor. These were divided among five sons, the others being given money. John, the eldest, was given Amble and Togston, and from him descended the families of the Cooks, who for some time resided at those places. Edward, the second son, born in 1711 had Blakemoor but lived in Newcastle. He was a barrister and antiquary. He was said to have at one time been in possession of the original copy of the Chartulary of Newminster Abbey, which in 1638 was one of the five Chartularies in the possession of Lord William Howard at Naworth Castle.

Mr. Cook had also copied from the records in the Chapel of Rolls, items pertaining to Northumberland. He had several lawsuits with the Cresswell family regarding right of seaweed on Broad Carr, but he failed to substantiate his claim. On his death he was succeeded by his brother George who, with his sister Isabella, also resided at Blakemoor (he must have moved from Newcastle at some time). Richard Cook, the third brother, born in 1719 died without issue. John Cook the youngest brother, born 1720, had three sons. The first, Edward, married Sarah Smetham and after her death he married Elizabeth Lawson. He lived at Southwick, County Durham, but after his Aunt Isabella's death he lived at Blakemoor where he died without issue. His wife was still there in 1829. John, the second son of John, married Dorothy Smethan, a cousin of his brother Edward's wife. He had three children, John, Sarah, and Margaret. By his aunt Isabella's will he had lands at Cresswell which he sold to Mr. Baker-Cresswell. George Cook married Mary Maule of Huntingdon.

The daughters of Edward Cook were Anne, Jane and Margaret. Jane married John Lawson, father of John Lawson late of Oldmoor and Cresswell. Isabella Cook the youngest child born 1723 left in her will of 1799, books, manuscripts, etc., to her niece Anne Lawson. The estate of Blakemoor and the east end of Cresswell to her nephew Edward Cook of Southwick, County Durham. Other estates in Cresswell were left to her sister, Jane Lawson. The remainder in fee simple to her nephew, John Cook, and a legacy of £500 to another nephew, George Cook. She also left £100 each to her four nieces, Anne, Dorothy, Margaret, and Elizabeth Cook.

The Cooks were still there in 1858 but in 1897 G. Moore is listed as being there and the sale of the Cresswell Estate in 1924 shows Messrs. Moore to be tenants, so it had been bought by the Cresswells after 1858. There are dates of birth for the four daughters of Edward Cook, but it earlier states that he had four sons and three daughters. This, I think, must be a printing error.

At the 1924 sale, Blakemoor was withdrawn but must have been subsequently sold to the Ashington Coal Company, then passed on to the N.C.B., and later leased to Alcan.

A nature trail from Alcan ends at Blakemoor where an outbuilding houses a small museum and rural life centre.

Ellington

The name of Ellington is derived from the Saxon meaning descendants of Ella and at various times it was also known as Ellinges and Elyngton.

Not much is known of its history until the reign of King John (1199-1216). The village was largely owned by Robert de Cresswell. Parts of it were, however, owned by various people through the centuries. One of the first owners of Ellington, of whom there is no direct evidence, was Sir Adam de Periton in 1242. And it was from this date that the Rev. John Hodgson starts his pedigree of the families who were connected with Ellington. However, it is possible to trace the history of succession to an earlier date. This has been set out in a paper read to the Newcastle Antiquarian Society on the 23rd of February, 1927, by G.G. Baker-Cresswell and H.H.E. Craster, D. Litt., F.S.A. It appears that the descent of land in Ellington passed through the families of Dumart, Vescy and Periton, to the de Welles, and it is of this last named family that the Rev. E.H.R. Tatham has worked out the following pedigree. It will be noticed that in this pedigree Sir William de Welles, who was Lord Chancellor of Ireland in 1451, was the last member of that family to prefix the 'de' before Welles.

Other people who held land in Ellington in this early period will be dealt with later. Although there were many owners, only a few acres were in the possession of these families in the early history of the village.

In addition to Ellington, Adam de Periton owned the manors of Faxton in Northamptonshire, and Oxhill in Warwickshire. These manors were inherited from the Dumart family. Alexander de Dumart was tenant of four bovates of land in Ellington, between 1197 and 1203, two of which he gave to Walter de Balliol and his heirs 'in fee'. This land was the equivalent of 60 acres and was held by Alden the son of Uethred. Norman, the son of Urskill, also held land in the village. Engelram de Dumart of Faxton and Oxhill owned land in Northumberland on which he paid a fine in 1178. There is no doubt that this land was in Ellington.

Engelram died in 1185 and left no children. His wife Maud, who survived him, had a share of her husband's estate in Faxton. His sisters and co-heirs, Emma and Alice, shared their brother's inheritance in 1201. There is no later record of Alice but Emma, who died in 1211, had a son Egelin who took his mother's name of Dumart. He died in 1219 and it is from that date that his nephew and heir succeeded to lands in Ellington and to the other estates. The name Periton is taken from Purton in Wiltshire which was one of his estates. He died in 1227 leaving a son and heir Adam de Periton. In 1234 Adam de Periton brought a lawsuit against Robert de Cresswell 'for customs and services due from the village of Cresswell'. In 1242-43 he was returned as holding Ellington, Cresswell, and Haydon of the Barony of Balliol by "one knights fee". He died in 1266 leaving no male issue. His three daughters were co-heirs of the previously mentioned estates which included Ellington. It was thus split into three parts but his daughter Margaret and her husband William de Kaynes had predeceased him and their son Robert was a minor at that time. The surviving daughters were Isabel widow of Sir Robert de Welles and Katherine wife of Sir John Paynel. After his coming of age Robert de Kaynes gave his share of Ellington to his aunt Isabel and to her second husband Sir William de Vescy. In return the Vescys gave their nephew a share in two of the Wiltshire manors. Isabel de Vescy thus became owner of two thirds of Ellington after the death of her husband in 1298. Her successor Adam, the third Lord de Welles, held the same amount of land when he died in 1345 and his son and heir John, who died in 1361, was the first of his line to own the whole of the manor of Ellington. It can be presumed that

TABLE I

Sir Robert de Welles II, living 1262 (Dodsworth MS. 49, f. 93); = Isabel, daughter and co-heir of Sir Adam de Periton, died before 1265   *d.* 1315; buried in Malton priory (*Linc. Notes and Queries* vi, 57)

Sir William de Welles III; a minor at his father's death; married Helwise (Harl. Ch. 57, G. 5); died before 1290 (*Abbrev. Plac.*, p. 223)

Sir Adam de Welles I, summoned = Joan Engayne, to parliament as 1st lord Welles, died 1316 1299-1311; died 1311; (*Cal. Inq.* (*Cal. Inq.* v, v, p. 200); buried in Greenfield p. 366, vi, p. priory (*Reg. Pal. Dun* ii, p. 780) 92); buried in Greenfield priory (*Linc. Notes and Queries* vi, 57)

Cecily   Aline

Sir Robert de Welles III, 2nd lord Welles; = Maud, sister and co-heir born 1297; proof of age, 1319 (*Cal. Inq.* of Richard de Clare, vi, p. 118); died 1320 (*Cal. Inq.* vi, p. 157) (*Cal. Inq.* vi, p. 159); died in or before 1327 (*Cal. Fine Rolls*, iv, p. 35)

Sir Adam de Welles II; = Margaret, born 1304; made proof died in her of age, 1326 (*Cal. Fine* husband's Rolls, iii, p. 410); sum- lifetime; moned to parliament buried in as 3rd lord Welles, Greenfield 1332-43; died 1345 priory (*Cal. Inq.* viii, p. 432); will dated 24th Feb. 1344/5; buried in Greenfield priory

Sir John de Welles

Sir John de Welles I; born 1334; proof of age, 1355; = Maud, stated to be daughter of (*Cal. Inq.* x, p. 232); summoned to parliament as William, lord Ross of Ham- 4th lord Welles, 1357-60; died 1361 (*Inq. p.m.*, 35 lake; died 1389 (*Inq. p.m.*, 12 Edw. III, pars 2, no. 81) Ric. II, no. 57)

---

(1) Cecily = **Sir John de Welles II**; born 1351; made proof of age = (2) Eleanor, daughter of John, = (3) Margaret, stated to 1373 (*Cal. Close Rolls*, 1369-74, p. 500); summoned to lord Mowbray, and earl be daughter of parliament as 5th lord Welles, 1376-1421; died 1421 of Nottingham Thomas, lord (*Inq. p.m.* 9 Hen. VI, no. 61) Ross; died 1424 (*Inq. p.m.* 4 Hen. VI, no. 30)

Eudo de Welles, died in his father's lifetime = Maud, daughter of Ralph, lord Greystoke   Other issue

Sir William de Welles, lord chancellor of Ireland, 1451-2

---

(1) Joan, daughter and co-heir = **Sir Leo or Lionel de Welles**; born 1406; = Margaret, daughter and heiress of of Sir Robert Waterton made proof of age, 1427-28; summoned Sir John Beauchamp of Bletsoe, of Methley (*Inq. p.m.* to parliament as 6th lord Welles, 1432-60; and widow of Sir Oliver St. John 15 Edw. IV, no. 45); lord lieutenant of Ireland, 1438-42; knight and of John Beauchamp, duke of buried in Methley of the Garter, 1457; slain in the battle of Somerset (*Inq. p.m.* 22 Edw. IV, church Towton, 29th March, 1461, and attainted no. 7) (*Inq. p.m.* 1 Edw. IV, no. 32); buried in Methley church

---

(1) Joan, daughter = **Sir Richard Welles**; born *c.* 1426; summoned to = (2) Margery, daughter and heiress of parliament as 7th lord Willoughby, *jure* of Sir James Robert, 6th lord *uxoris*, 1454; had his father's estates restored Strangeways and Willoughby of to him in 1465; restored to his father's peerage widow of John Eresby (Fine Roll, as 7th lord Welles in 1468; executed 12th Ingleby; married 31 Hen. VI, m. March, 1470; his honours attainted, 1475 in 1466 (*Testamenta* 1; *Inq. p.m.* 1 (*Inq. p.m.* 15 Edw. IV, no. 47) *Eboracensia* III, p. Edw. IV, no. 33) 339); had Ellington manor for life; took the veil, 8th May, 1475

Eleanor Cecily Margaret Katherine (see Table II)

Sir Robert Welles IV; born *c.* 1433; leader = Elizabeth, daughter of John of the Lincolnshire rebellion of 1470; Bourchier, lord Berners; executed 19th March, 1470, and attainted will dated 2nd Oct., 1470 with his father; *s.p.*; buried in the church (*North Country Wills*, of White Friars, Doncaster p. 34); buried at White Friars, Doncaster.

Joan, married 1st Richard Pygot and 2ndly Sir Richard Hastings, K.G., who had restitution of the Welles and Willoughby estates and was summoned to parliament as 8th lord Welles and Willoughby *jure uxoris*, 1482-3 and died *s.p.* 1503; will dated 19th March, 1504/5; proved 1505 (*North Country Wills*, p. 73); buried in the church of Grey Friars, London

---

John Welles, had the Welles estates and barony restored to him = Lady Cecily Plantagenet, daughter of King Edward IV; in 1485; summoned to parliament as viscount Welles, 1st married 2ndly Thomas Kyme, of the Isle of Wight, Sept., 1487; made knight of the Garter in 1488; died 9th Feb., and died 24th Aug., 1507, aged 38; buried in Quarr 1498/9; will dated 8th Feb., 1498/9 (*North Country Wills*, p. 63); abbey buried in Westminster Abbey

---

Elizabeth, died in her father's lifetime   Anne, died *circa* 1500; buried in the Austin Friars, London

TABLE II

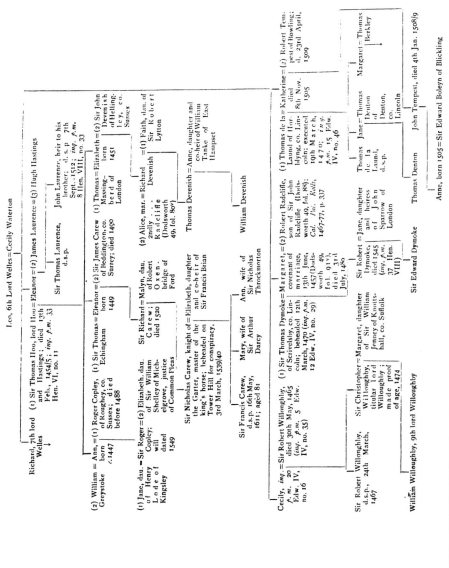

Leo, 6th Lord Welles=Cecily Waterton

Katherine Paynel's third share was not acquired by the de Welles' family before the middle of the 14th century. However, descent in the intervening years has not been traced.

William de Vescy, who was the second husband of Isabel de Periton, was the younger brother of John de Vescy, Lord of Alnwick, whom he succeeded in 1289. His claim to the throne of Scotland was dubious. Had it been otherwise Isabel would have been queen of Scots. After the death of her husband, Isabel inherited the dower of her two husbands as well as her own lands in Ellington and Faxton. She gave a third part of Faxton to her daughter-in-law, Clemence de Vescy, widow of John de Vescy who was her only son by her second husband. And to her daughters by her first marriage, Cecily and Aline de Welles, she gave £20 rent out of the remaining two thirds of Faxton and a life tenancy of Ellington. She died in 1315 and was succeeded by her grandson, Sir Robert de Welles. At this point it is worth mentioning that the de Welles estate was succeeded by a minor on five successive occasions. When John, the fourth Lord de Welles, came of age in 1355, the 'escheator' for Northumberland ordered Robert and Roger de Cresswell to give him the lands which they possessed in Ellington. Sir John de Welles served under Henry Percy, Earl of Northumberland, in the reign of Richard II. It is recorded that he fought a duel with David, Earl of Crawford, and the episode is related by Dugdale from Stowe. "Lord John de Welles was sent as ambassador to Scotland, to treat concerning certain matters of great importance betwixt both Kings, he happened to be at a solemn banquet, where the Scots and English were discoursing of deeds of arms, and said, 'let words have no place, if ye know not the chivalry and valiant deeds of Englishmen, appoint me a day and place when ye list and ye shall have experience'. Where unto David Earl of Crawford assenting this, John de Welles chose London Bridge for the place, the Earl of Crawford assigned St. George's day for the time. Upon the day of the battle both of them coming to the bridge on their barbed horses, at the sound of the trumpet, encountered each other with square grouden spears, in which Earl David sat so strong that, notwithstanding the spear was broken on his helmit and visage, he stirred not, insomuch that the spectators cried out that, contrary to the law of arms he was bound to the saddle. 'Whereupon he dismounted and got up again and run a second course, but in the third, he threw this John de Welles out of his saddle to the ground, and dismounting again embraced him, that the people might understand he had no hatred towards him and with great humanity visited him afterwards every day till he recovered his health'. John de Welles was summoned to Parliament from 1357-1422, following in the footsteps of his forebears who had also served in Parliaments under different Kings. He died in 1422 owning lands in Ellington and elsewhere.

The descent of Leo the 6th Lord de Welles can be traced in the pedigree. He was born in 1406 and his second wife was the dowager Duchess of Somerset. Through this marriage, he became connected with the reigning House of Lancaster. Fighting for that cause in the Wars of the Roses he was killed at the battle of Towton Field in 1461. He had been summoned to Parliament in 1432-60 and held the office of Lord Lieutenant of Ireland in 1438-42, and was made a Knight of the Garter in 1457. Having supported the Opposition his lands were forfeited to the Crown and later granted to Robert Lord Ogle.

Lord Ogle only held the land for three and half years, because in 1456 Sir Richard Welles the eldest son of the 6th Lord de Welles had his father's estates restored to him. He was summoned to Parliament in 1465-66 under the title of Lord Willoughby, but in 1470 he was beheaded by Edward IV for his complicity in the Lincolnshire Rebellion. His son, Robert Welles (note: Hodgson's pedigree has Richard and not Robert) suffered a similar fate when he attempted to avenge his father's death.

The Welles' estates thus became forfeited for a second time although were not included in the formal act of attainder until 1475. That act gave to Dame Margery the widow of the 7th Lord Welles a life tenancy in the Manor of Ellington in compensation for an annuity out of two Lincolnshire properties. The same act secured the life interests of Margaret Duchess of Somerset and Maud, Lady Willoughby, in other estates and settled the remainder of the Welles' lands for life upon Sir Richard Hastings who had married Joan, the only surviving child and heir of the 7th Lord Welles. On March 16th, 1475 the revisions of the Welles' estate including that of the Manor of Ellington on the death of Lady Welles were granted to Richard Duke of York, the younger of the "Princes in the Tower". The reason for this revision was that Lady Welles entered a nunnery. This would have annulled her life interest in Ellington thereby causing its return to the Crown.

With the overthrow of the House of York at Bosworth Field in 1485, the Welles family once more came into favour. Its last male representative, John Welles – half brother and male heir of the 7th Lord Welles, had his father's estates restored to him and was created a baron and later a viscount. He also married Princess Cecily, daughter of King Edward IV and sister of Henry VII's Queen, thus becoming brother-in-law to the King.

Viscount Welles died in 1499 and in 1503 another act of Parliament was passed, limiting the succession to his estates. Provision was made that his widow should hold the lands for life with certain exceptions. After her death the land should revert to the King for a period of ten years, after which they should be divided between the heirs of the four daughters of the 6th Lord Welles.

From here on the succession of the estate becomes somewhat confused through the marriages of the four daughters and the subsequent division of the estate. So, at this point it would be best for the reader to consult the pedigree. However, a later period is worthy of note, because it refers to Sir Francis Carew, who inherited a 9th part of the manor of Ellington. He died in 1520 leaving a son and heir, Sir Nicholas Carew who was a Knight of the Garter and Master of the Horse to Henry VIII. He was executed for high treason in 1539 for having engaged in a conspiracy to set the Marquis of Exeter on the throne.

His lands were forfeited but restored in 1553 to his son and heir, Francis Carew, who in 1573 gave his portion of the Manor of Ellington and other property to Arthur Hall of Doncaster. With the completion of the descent of the de Welles family, other owners of land in Ellington can now be shewn.

In the reign of King John, Robert de Balliol gave 12 acres of land to Walter, the son of Philip of Linton. In 1240 by a deed, probably issued about that time, Beatrice Pawlyne of Ellington, in her widowhood, gave to Robert son of Walter of Ellington "that toft of land between her own ground and that of William Byker" and half a rood of land adjoining the park between the grounds of Ralph son of Tymoth and those of William Byker.

In 1294 the prior of St. John of Jerusalem Hospital possessed land for which he claimed various immunities.

Agnes Graper who died in 1343 owned land in Ellington and in the reign of Edward III and Richard I John de Wendout and his heirs held a messuage and 18 acres of land. This appears by a number of inquests after their deaths.

In 1360 Edward III granted lands to John Hunter for the sum of ten marks. This also included tenements in Hurst, Newbiggin, Ellington and elsewhere, which had belonged to John de Horsley and John Thorald, adherents to Gilbert Middleton in his revolt against Edward II.

A writ was issued in 1377 respecting lands in Ellington and other places and this was granted to the priory of Tynemouth.

In 1422 Sir Ralph Eure, heir of William Vescy, whose family had intermarried with the Vescys and the Aytons, died leaving interests in the village and also in Hayden and Lynemouth. Hayden is unknown today but was once part of the manor of Ellington and in the Barony of Balliol. In 1240 it belonged to Adam de Periton from whom it descended to the families of Vescy and Welles. There is a Haydon Letch near East Moor Farm on the local map and John Hodgson suggests that the site may have been where Dene House is situated on the bank of the River Lyne between Ellington and Lynemouth.

Hallywell is also mentioned as being one of the manors of this Parish that were in the Barony of Balliol, which was situated between Earsdon and Seaton Deleval.

There was a writ issued in the reign of Henry VI respecting messuages in Alnwick, eight in Warkworth and two in Ellington, which had been granted to the chaplain of the chantry of the Blessed Virgin in Alnwick by Henry Earl of Northumberland.

In the reign of Elizabeth I there was a decree in a suit in the exchequer for the tenants to enjoy Aldenfield (the site of which is not known) for ever by paying 20/- a year to the Queen and the same sum to the defendant in the suit.

The indexes to the Recorder of the Auditor of Land Revenue refer to grants of tenements in the village same reign to Reginald Brisco and Henry Haggerston and to 14 other deeds and records respecting property in Ellington.

The Widdrington family acquired land in Ellington at an early period of its history and Robert of Gloucester gave his son John a toft and a croft in "Hellington". John conveyed to Duncan de Widdrington a "toft" by deed for which there is no date and in the reign of Henry III Richard son of Robert of Gloucester gave a "toft" and three acres in Ellington to John, son of John de Widdrington. In the same period John, Lord Widdrington, gave to David Lasceles, who was married to his cousin Joan, all his lands with the "tofts" which he and his brother Duncan owned in Ellington. Edmund de Ellington, the son of Ralph de Stokys, gave to Duncan de Widdrington ½ acre of land in the village.

In 1367, Isabella, daughter and heir of Robert Darayns, gave "seisin" to Roger de Widdrington all the lands in Ellington which she inherited from her father.

The possessions which the Widdringtons held in the parish continued throughout the feudal period and were part of the Barony of Balliol, which, from the time of Richard II to Elizabeth I when it was forfeited, belonged to the Nevilles of Raby. This family also held a "moiety" of Lynemouth and Hurst, in fee of the crown, as well as possessions in Ellington, Cresswell, and Haydon.

In the reign of Henry VII, Sir Ralph de Widdrington gave to his chaplain William de Thornton, for his good services, all his lands and tenements which he held in Ellington. The property which the family had in the parish of Woodhorn in the time of Henry VI, after the death of Sir John Widdrington in 1444, consisted of the manor of Woodhorn, a fishing village on the Wansbeck, property in Newbiggin, two husbandlands and one cottage in Cresswell, three husbandlands and a cottage in Ellington, Newton near Ellington and a village in Linton. After the death of Lady Elizabeth Carey, the wife of Lord Robert Carey of Lippington, and widow of Sir Henry Widdrington, the Manor of Ellington was one of the possessions of the Widdringtons and must have remained so until after the death of Henry Widdrington in the reign of Elizabeth I. However, by 1633 there is no mention of their having possessions in Ellington.

In that year the recorded owners were William Brown, Matt Hall, William Swan, Thomas Corby, Margery Smith, John Fenwick, and John Ridley.

The above date, however, contradicts a later entry which states that Lord Widdrington forfeited the manor of Woodhorn, Ellington, Cresswell and Newbiggin in

PEDIGREE OF THE ASKEWS, PROPRIETORS OF ELLINGTON AND LINTON,

[This name was originally *Ake-skeugh*, which signifies Oak-knoll, or hilly ground covered with wood. They were descended from Thruston of the Wood (Thrustanus de Bosco), who lived in the time of king John, and had feoffment from the Boyvils, lords of Kirksanton, of a place called *Akeskeugh*, within the lordship of Millum, in Cumberland, from which place they derived their name. The authorities for the former part of this pedigree will be found in Burn and Nicholson's History of Westmorland, p. 255; and the latter part of it was communicated to the author by Richard Craster Askew, esq. of Newcastle upon Tyne.]

I.—Sir Hugh Askew, knight, who was descended from Thruston de Bosco, and raised to great honours and preferment for his services to king Henry the Eighth, had a gift of the nunnery of Seaton, which is about four miles south of Mulcaster, in Cumberland, and was then worth £500 a year. He had been yeoman of the cellar to queen Catharine, but upon her divorce lost his situation; but had it restored by a dexterous manoeuvre. " He applied himself to the lord chamberlain for some place or other in the king's service. The lord chamberlain knew him well, because he had helped him to a cup of the best; but told him he had no place for him but that of a charcoal carrier. ' Well,' quoth Askew, ' help me in with one foot, and let me get the other in as I can.' And upon a great holiday, the king, looking out at some sports, Askew got a courtier (a friend of his) to stand beside the king, and he got on his velvet cassock and his gold chain, and a basket of coal on his back, and marched in the king's sight with it. ' O,' says the king, ' now I like yonder fellow well that disdains not to do his dirty office in his dainty clothes—what is he?' Says his friend that stood by on purpose : ' It is Mr Askew, that was yeoman of the cellar to the late queen's majesty, and is now glad of this poor place, to keep him in your majesty's service, which he will not forsake for all the world.' The king says : ' I had the best wine when he was in the cellar; he is a gallant wine taster; let him have his place again.'" In l Edw. VI. and 3 Eliz. he was sheriff of Cumberland; and for his bravery and good conduct at the battle of Musselburgh, was created a knight banneret under the royal standard in the camp at Roxburgh. His tombstone in Millum church bears the following inscription :—" Here lyeth Sir Hughe Asketh, knight, late of the seller to king Edward the VI. : which Sir Hughe was mald knight at Muskelbroughfelde in the yere of oure Lord 1547, and died the second day of Marche in the year of oure lord 1562."

..... , daur. of John Huddleston, of Millum Castle, in the county of Cumberland, one of whose wives was Joan, sister to sir John Seymour, father of the lady Jane Seymour, third wife of Henry the Eighth.

II.—Hugh Askew, of Greymanes, in the parish of Mulcaster, in the county of Cumberland. Some think that this Hugh was nephew to Hugh the cellarer.

III.—Henry Askew, of Greymanes, died, according to the parish register of Mulcaster, in 1621.

IV.—William Askew, who sold Greymanes, and purchased an estate at Kirkby, in coun. of Lancaster, and died in 1641.

V.—John Askew, of Kirkby, in the county of Lancaster.

VI.—Anthony Askew, of Kendal, M. D., second son.══Anne, only daur. of Adam Storrs, of Storrshall, in coun. Lancaster.

VII.—Adam Askew, of Newcastle upon Tyne, M. D., where he settled about the year 1725, and soon fell into very extensive practice. In 1750, he purchased the lands in Ellington and Linton forfeited by lord Widdrington in 1715, and died in 1773.══Anne, a younger daur. and co-heir of Richard Crakenthorpe, of Newbigging, in the county of Westmorland.

Anthony. Margaret.

VIII.—1. Margaret,═1. Anthony Askew, M.D. justly celebrated for his extensive collection of books & manuscripts, especially such as were connected with Greek literature. He was born at Kendal in 1722; of Emanuel College, Cambridge, B.M. 1745; studied at Leyden; and accompanied the English embassy to Constantinople: took the degree of M. D. June 3, 1750. He died at Hampstead, in 1784; after which his collection of books and manuscripts sold for upwards of £5000.—(*See Gentleman's Magazine*, 1784.) | 2. Elizabeth, daur. of Robert Halford, esq., a master in chancery. She died in 1778. | 2. Adam Askew, A. M., rector of Plumland, in Cumberland, the perpetual advowson of which living his father, 22 Oct. 1765, purchased of the duke of Portland for £1300. His father also purchased Middleton Hall, in the parish of Kirby Lonsdale, and left it to this Adam. | 1. Deborah, died at the age of 19, unmarried. 2. Anne died in 1813, unmarried.

3. Henry Askew, M. D., practised for about three time as a physician. He married Dorothy, daur. of Adam Boultby, of Whitby, esq., and died in 1796. s. p. His widow died in 1792. They were both bur. in St John's church, Newcastle.
4. John Askew, esq. of Pallinsburn and Goswick, by his will, dated 21 September, 1794, left the caste of Berwick, the Mills, and the estate of Castle Hills, to his wife, for life; his lands at Holy Island to his son William; and to his eldest son Geo. Adam, the silver jar given to him by lord Monthermer, to go with Pallinsburn as an heir loom.—(*Raine's Test.* 833.)

Bridget, only child of John Watson, esq. of Goswick.

IX.—1. Adam Askew, of═Amy, daur. of Greythough, in the coun. of Durham, and of Wimpole Street, London, esq.; created patentee high sheriff of the coun. pal. of Durham in 1809, on the death of sir Hedworth Williamson.
daur. of Robert Carey, a merchant in London.

2. Anthony Linacre Askew, M. A., was fellow of King's College, Cambridge; died unmarried in 1818.
3. Henry Askew, in holy orders, rector of Greystock, in Cumberland, marr. Anne, daur. of Thomas Sunderland, esq. of Ulverstone, in coun. of Lancaster, by whom he has issue—Henry, Anne, and Ellen.
4. Richard Askew, esq. was formerly a major in the 27th regiment of infantry, from which he has retired on half-pay.
5. Thomas Askew, esq.══Lucy, youngest daur. of Robert Carey, of London aforesaid, and sister of the wife of her husband's eldest brother.

1. Anne Elizabeth.═1. George Adam Askew, of Pallinsburn and Goswick, esq. eldest son and heir.
2. Sarah died about the year 1809, unmarried.
3. Deborah married Sir Lucas Pepys, bt. M. D., and physician to his late Majesty George the Third, and has no issue.
4. Amy married the Rev. John Washington, of Winchester, and had issue—Henry, a clergyman, who is dead, s. p.; John, a lieut. in the army; Adam, a barrister; Elizabeth, and Maria.
6. Mary died in 1784, unmarried.
5. Elizabeth.══Henry Percy Pulleine, of Carleton Hall, in Yorkshire.

2. Elizabeth Anne.
3. John Watson, in holy orders; fellow of University College; will dated January 19, 1805 (*Raine's Test.* 846); died in 1810.
4. Sir Henry, K.C.B., a major-general in the army.
5. William was first lieutenant of the Triumph, 74 guns, and was killed by an accident on board in 1806.
6. Isabella unmarried.
7. Richard Craster, a barrister in Newcastle upon Tyne, to whom the author is indebted for contributions to this pedigree.
8. Christopher Crackenthorpe, a captain in R. N.
9. Hugh Bertram, a retired officer in the naval service of the East India Company.

Elizabeth.
Thomas.
John.
Lucy.
Georgiana.

1. Henry, a cornet in the first regiment of dragoons; now dead.
2. Elizabeth Dorothea.
3. Henrietta married ...... Hinks, a capt. in the horse artillery.
4. James.
5. Anne, wife of the Rev. Mr Ryder, of ......, near Sheffield.

6. Frances.
7. Amy.
8. Robert.
9. Sarah.
10. Charlotte.

FROM :- Hodgson ,John. History of Northumberland. Pt II. Vol II.1832. pp.198-9.

52

1715. No reason is given for the forfeiture. In 1682, Martin Ogle, who had spent 30 years in Virginia, America, conveyed his estate in Ellington to William Ogle of Causey Park. An undated entry lists Thomas de Aukeland, parson of Whalton, as being granted messuage, land and rent in Ellington.

In 1750, land in the village was advertised for sale having "a free rent" of £2.11.2d annually and Denehouse was let at £374.16.0d. After the failure of the York Building Company to complete their purchase of these lands, the greater part of them were sold to Adam Askew M.D. of Newcastle. He died in 1773 leaving his property in Ellington to his nephew Adam Askew of Redheugh in the county of Durham who still had possessions in Ellington in 1830.

However, by 1830 the greater part of the village was owned by the Cresswells and remained so until the sale of the whole estate in 1924 (see sale list). Although all the farms were not sold at that time, they did eventually come into the possession of the Ashington Coal Company. The names of these farms can be seen in the sale list. The name of Askew is an ancient one and was originally Ake-skeugh which means Oak-knoll or Hilly ground covered with woods. They were descended from Thruston of the Wood (Thrustanus de Bosco) who lived in the reign of King John and had feoffment from the Boyvills Lords of Kirksanton and of the place named Akeskeugh within the Lordship of Millum in Cumbria, hence the name.

Sir Hugh Askew received rewards for his services under Henry VIII. He was Yeoman of the Cellar (wine) to Queen Catherine, but after her divorce, lost his position.

The following is an account of how it was regained:—

"He applied himself for help to the Lord Chamberlain for some place or other in the King's service. The Lord Chamberlain knew him well because he had helped him to a cup of the best; but told him he had no place for him but that of charcoal wood carrier. "Well", quoth Askew, "Help me in with one foot and let me get the other in as I can."

"Upon a great holiday, the King was looking out at some sports. Askew got a cortier friend of his to stand beside the King, and he got on his velvet cassock and his gold chain, and a basket of coal on his back, and marched to the King's sight with it. 'Oh!' says the King, 'Now I like yonder fellow that distains not to do his dirty office in his dainty clothes – what is he?' Says his friend that stood by on purpose: It is Mr. Askew that was Yeoman of the Cellar to the late Queen, Majesty, and is glad of this poor place to keep him in your Majesty's service, which he will not forsake for all the World. The King says I had the best wine when he was in the cellar; he is a gallant wine taster, let him have his place again". In Edward VI and Elizabeth I's reigns, he was sheriff of Cumberland and for his bearing and good conduct at the Battle of Musselburgh was created a knight under the Royal Standard in the camp at Roxburgh. His tombstone in Millum church bears the inscription "Here lyeth Sir Hugh Askew, knight, later of the cellar to King Edward VI which Sir Hugh was made knight at Muskelbroughfiede in the year of our Lord 1547, and died the second day of March in the yere of oure lord 1562".

Ellington
The 19th and 20th Centuries

The Hallowell family has been prominent in the village for many years, arriving there in 1802 from Holywell from whence they took their name, having come from

Scotland. Mr. W. Hallowell, who died in 1984, lived in the cottage which they occupied when first coming to the village.

They established a wheelwrights, coachbuilders and carpentry business and they were also undertakers. With the demise of horsedrawn vehicles, a coachbuilding business was established in Ashington, where it has only recently passed out of the hands of the family. In the last century, W.H. Hallowell constructed a waterwheel which was put into the nearby river and supplied water to the village. It was 1935 before the houses were connected to mains supply.

In 1821, the village had 52 houses and a population of 255. Most of the houses were occupied by labourers and craftsmen working on the erection of Cresswell Hall and its appurtenances.

There were two inns, the Plough and the Sun, the latter is not mentioned as being licensed after 1855. The greater part of the village was owned by the Baker-Cresswell's, until the sale of the estate in 1924. In 1912, a Co-operative store was built on land which was once a mason's yard for the Cresswell Estate. It was next to the building which had been the Sun Inn, opposite the Plough. The manager of the store, a Mr. J. Dixon, lived in this house to which a lean-to building had been added. This was the Drapery Department, managed by Maggie Morgan. Mr. Ralph Robson, who still lives in the village, was a grocery assistant. He had to travel to the surrounding villages and farms for grocery orders at the beginning of the week and these would be delivered by horse and wagon at the end of the week by Mr. J. Bell, the carter.

The building of a larger Co-operative Store at Lynemouth saw the demise of the one in Ellington. The premises then had a variety of uses over the years, including a garage, post office and general dealers which is what it is now. It is called the Bank Top Store and is owned by Mr. and Mrs. J. Robson. There was a small sweet-shop run by Mr. J. Barker in one of the small cottages, but it closed a few years ago. The smithy was along there too.

The big stone-built house was Ellington Farm House, once the abode of the farmer who farmed the land of that name on which the Highthorne Estate was built. An American named Mr. _ ady leased some of the farms from the N.C.B., but in 1963 this lease was transferred to Alcan. Some of the fields are used for growing cereals and others for grazing cattle.

Very little building had been done in the village until the 1970's, when the High-thorne Estate building started. There had been considerable discussion during the 1950's and 1960's by the Morpeth Council on a scheme called Broadline, which would in effect have made a mini-town, embracing the village and some of the surrounding area. Fortunately, this scheme was abandoned, as the completion of the Highthorne Estate has completely changed the character of what was once a rural village.

Recreation and Sport:

For several years, commencing in 1898, Juvenile sports were organised by Mr. Temple, licencee of the Plough Inn. Entrants were drawn from the surrounding villages for the Foot Races.

Many social functions took place in an Institute which was opened in 1908 by the Countess Ravensworth. The building, which has been a private residence for many years, is situated a little way past the Plough Inn, and is of yellowish brick.

In 1922 there was a branch of the Royal Ancient Order of Buffaloes.

In 1923, a football club was formed and it was still going until the outbreak of the war, but was not revived after the end of hostilities. It was in the Ashington Welfare League.

In 1924, the Rev. Horsfall opened a Recreation Hall, which was in fact an ex-army hut. It was opposite Hubbs Garage. The Miners' Institute, or Ellington Welfare Social Centre as it is now called, was opened in 1924. It is still the venue for many of the societies which now flourish in the village.

The Ellington Colliery Brass Band has flourished for many years, many of its members being drawn from Lynemouth. For many years Mrs. Statham staged plays in the Institute, and in 1937 there was a performance of "Babes in the Wood" with the following cast:— John O'Keefe – Bellman, Walter Bell – Robin Hood, Bobby Horn – Wicked Uncle, Edna Railston – Schoolmistress, Doris Bell – Fairy Queen, Willie Routledge, Eileen Smith – Babes, Margaret Scott, Pat Stoker and Peggy Marriot played robins. Margaret Grieves – Wicked Aunt, Ella Strachan – Puck, Charles Kerr, John Marriot, Stanley Brown, N. Marriot, O. Scott, G. Horn, J. Tate, A. Bell and W. Rogerson were bandits. M. Statham, A Downie, N. Routledge, E. Prior, G. French, E. Mitchell, and Bella Marriot were fairies.

There are darts teams in the Stobswood League and the Plough Inn is represented in the East Coquetdale League.

List of Societies

Ellington Colliery Institute
Women's Institute
Youth Club
Ladies Club
Pre-school Play Group
Brownies
District Community Committee
Horticultural Society
Darby and Joan Club
Northumberland Radio Club
Floral Art Club
Ellington Colliery Band
Scout Troup

Militia List – 1762

Able bodied men between 16 & 60 yrs.

Thomas Saint	Farmer
George Dunn	Servant
Robert Ogell	Farmer
Thomas Scott	Barnman
James Brown	Daytalisman
John Allen	Daytalisman
Edward Swan	Farmer
Matthew Lawson	Single. Servant
George Cook	Single. Servant
John Davison	Single. Servant
Lance Fenwick	Master Tailor
Thomas Scott	Journeyman Tailor
Mark Forster	Fish Carrier
John Stirling	Fish Carrier
John Pearson	Single. Servant

John Spoures	Master Tailor
John Spoures	Son of above
Thomas Anderson	Hind
Thomas Davison	Barnman
G. Dixon	Weaver
W. Crake	Farmer
G. Atchtion	Nurseryman
Andrew Shanks	Fish Carrier
Ralph Veres	Blacksmith
John Paten	Servant
George Shanks	Farmer
Thomas Hedely	Ploughwright
Robert Bowmar	Lame, and thought to be above age
Ambrose Richinson	Farmer (Dene House)
Anton Richinson	Hind (Dene House)
William Heddley	Farmer (East and West Moor Farms)
Thomas Thompson	Farmer (East and West Moor Farms)
Thomas Reviley	Hind (East and West Moor Farms)
Andrew Akine	Hind (East and West Moor Farms)
Lyonell Tindle	Petty Constable
John Tindle	Son of above
William Domison	Hind
William Rennison	Hind
Patrick Smith	Servant
John Humphrey	Petty Constable

Both Military and Posse Comitatus lists were drawn up in order to provide a reserve of manpower to supress riots and invasion. The country at that time was at war with France (Wagons and horses were included). All these would have been placed at the command of the Army and Sheriff of the county.

J. Scott	J. Robson
Jas. Doobion	T. Glaf
G. Hudson	Andrew Rearvely
Alex Davidson	T. Bulmer
Henry Bowie	K. Frewster
R. Glaf	W. Cowsey
Bart Donaldson	T. Purvis
E. Purvis	G. Turnbull
J. Lamb	G. Brown
J. Creighton (Dene House)	A. Richardson (Dene House)
R. Wood (Hagg House)	J. Wood (Hagg House)
T. Scott	J. Proudlock
A. Thornton	W. Johnson
W. Tate (Highthorne)	W. Barn (Highthorne)
A. Weldon (Highthorne)	H. Weldon (Highthorne)
Antony Weldon (Highthorne)	John Dunn (Highthorne)
John Scrapton (West Moor)	Jos. Reed (West Moor)
Thomas Dodds (West Moor)	J. Day (East Moor)
E. Brown (East Moor)	John Richardson (Constable)

Transport for militia and goods in the event of invasion or riot, under command of the Sheriff.

Carts	Carthorses	
John Wood, Hagg House	6	13
John Fenwick, Highthorne	6	12
Amos Richardson, Ellington	6	13
James Anderson, West Moor, Ellington	2	4
W. Sedgwick, West Moor	2	4
T. Gifford, East Moor	1	4
W. Shanks	1	2
T. Hedley	1	2
J. Shanks	1	2
W. Brown	1	2
J. Purvis	2	5
R. Robson	1	4
Jos. Hair	1	2
Andrew Shanks	1	2
W. Temple (Jnr.)	1	–
J. Stevenson	1	–
R. Harbottle	1	–
W. Hallowell	1	–
G. Dixon	1	–
TOTAL	37	71

Ellington Trade Directories

Pearson and White – 1828

W. Athey, Schoolmaster.
T. Bell, Farmer, High Thorne.
G. Gustard, Blacksmith.
Ann Gutherson, Grocer.
Stephen Gutherson, Cartwright and Joiner.
Jacob Hill, Farmer.
Thomas Hallowell, Cartwright and Joiner.
W. Hallowell, Plough Inn.
W. Jewsey, Tailor.
T. Purvis, Farmer.
J. Shanks, Sunn Inn (opposite the Plough, now a private residence).
J. Stephenson, Shoemaker and grocer.
J. Taylor, Gamekeeper.
T. Thew, Miller.

Whites Directory – 1847

W. Adam, Schoolmaster.
P. Allison, Miller.
T. Bell, Farmer.
Rev. Goldsmith.
Cath Gutterson, Plough Inn.
Thos. Hallowell, Cartwright.
J. Hudspath, Gardener.
Thos. Johnson, Blacksmith.
W. Jewsey, Tailor.
T. Purvis, Farmer (East Moor Farm).
J. Shanks, Shoemaker and licencee of Sun Inn.
Willis and Bell, Farmers (West Moor).
J. Wray, Shopkeeper.

Whites Directory – 1855

Peter Allison, Farmer and Miller.
T. Bell, Farmer (East Moor Farm).
W. Bell, Farmer, Highthorne.
T. Hallowell, Joiner and Cartwright.
T. Johnson, Blacksmith.
J. & W. Oliver, Tailors and Drapers.
John Shanks, Licencee, Sun Inn.
R. Taylor, Stonemason.
Thomas Wray, Shopkeeper and Shoemaker.

Bulmers Directory – 1887

John Watson, Postmaster and Grocer.
William Hallowell, Joiner and Cartwright.
John Marshall, Blacksmith and licencee of Plough Inn.
John Pringle, Enginewright.
Ralph Robson, Woodman.
Robert Robson, Stonemason.

Kelly's Directory – 1902

Rev. Horsfall.
A. Cirney, Ellington Farm.
Jane Finley, Post Office.
Thomas Hallowell, Joiner and Cartwright.
Anthony Robson, Postman.
Joseph Robson, Farmer (East Moor Farm).
R. Smith, Stonemason.
R. Scott, Blacksmith.
T. Stamp, Dene House and Highthorne Farm.
W. Stoker, Ellington Mill Farm.
Thomas Temple, Plough Inn.
F. Wetheral, Schoolmaster.
Mr. E. Wood, Hagg Farm.

Ellington
1910

Same as 1901, plus –
G. Herson, Organist and Choirmaster.
G. Marvin, Secretary of Colliery Institute.
R. Marvin, Blacksmith.
T. Robson, Farm Steward, Ashington Coal Co. (West Moor Farm).
J. Linton and J. Chester, Overseers, Whittles, Linton Mill.

1925

W. Clark, Garden House.
Davison, East Moor Farm.
W. Ellerington, Manager, West Moor Farm, and Blakemoor Farm.
Jane Finley, Post Office.
E. Hallowell and Son, Joiners.
R. Marvin, Blacksmith and Farmer.
Jesse Robinson, Shopkeeper.
Isabella Taylor, Ellington Mill.
Thos. Woodrow, Plough Inn.

1929

T. Bell, Shopkeeper.
Jas. Davidson, East Moor Farm.
J. Elliott, West Moor Farm.
E. Hallowell & Sons, Joiners.
R. Marvin, Blacksmith and Farmer.
G. Clark, Plough Inn.
W. Scott, Motor Garage.
R. Sisterson, Ellington Farm.
F. Stamp, Highthorne.
A. Todd, Ellington Mill.
Joseph Wood, Hagg Farm.

1934

Rev. Tause.
T. Bell, Shopkeeper.
R. Grieve, Farmer.
Adam Hindmarsh, Farm Steward, Ashington Coal Co., Highthorne.
G. Proudlock, Haulage Co.
G. Steel, Steward, Ashington Coal Co., West Moor Farm.
R. Sisterson, Ashington Coal Co., Ellington Farm.
W. Tiplady, Plough Inn.
A. Todd, Ellington Mill.
Matt Tough, Farm Manager.
Addison Wood, Hagg Farm.
Linton – Mrs. May Carmichael, Ashington Coal Co., N & S Farm.

1841 Census

In 1841 all parishes were required to take a census of all residents. Previously, births, marriages and deaths were all recorded in the church registers.

Name	Age	Occupation
Robert Wallace	30	Agricultural Labourer
Margaret Wallace	30	Wife
Mary Wallace	7	
Margaret Wallace		
Isabella Wallace	4	Children
John Wallace	1	
Jane Burn	15	Servant
Thomas Maughan	35	Teacher
John Dixon	45	Labourer
Sara Dixon	40	Spinster
Stephen Gutherson	65	Cartwright
Cath Gutherson	20	Wife
Margaret Gutherson	3	
Cath Gutherson	1	Children
John Hall	15	Cartwright (Apprentice)
Margery Atkinson	14	Servant
Thomas Johnson	45	Blacksmith
Elizabeth Johnson	50	Wife
Jane Heir	20	
Jane Brewis	20	
Isabella Murton	20	
Roger Potts	20	Journeyman
Richard Nelson	20	Journeyman
Thomas Robson	15	Blacksmith (Apprentice)
G. Purvis	70	Farmer
Margery Purvis	60	Wife
Jane Arkle	20	Servant
Margery Arkle	18 mnths	
Jane Mills	25	Servant
Peter Allison	45	Miller Ellington Mill
Margery Allison	35	Wife Ellington Mill
Peter Allison	20	Miller Ellington Mill
John Allison	15	Ellington Mill
James Allison	15	Ellington Mill
Ralph Allison	15	Ellington Mill
Peter Allison	15	Ellington Mill
John Allison	4	Ellington Mill
Ann Allison	15	Ellington Mill
Elizabeth Allison	8	Ellington Mill
Isobella Allison	6	Ellington Mill
Alice Elrington	15	Servant
John Shanter	65	Inn Keeper
John Shanter	30	Shoemaker
Will Shanter	25	
Margaret Shanter	20	

Mary Mather	15	
Adam Young	30	Shepherd
Rachel Young	30	Wife
Will Young	5	
Robert Young	6 mnths	
Elizabeth Rochester	20	Servant
Andrew Shanks	75	Parish
Kath Shanks	75	Parish
Mary Beveridge	45	Parish
Mary Beveridge	8	Parish
William Riddell	67	Woodman
Mary Riddell	62	Wife
John Hudspith	55	Gardener
Mary Hudspith	55	Wife
Robert Hudspith	35	Mason
Mary Hudspith	15	
William Frost	30	Mounted Coastguard
Ann Frost	25	Wife
Mary Frost	15	
W. Jowsey	70	Tailor
Alice Jowsey	65	Wife
Will Jowsey	20	Journeyman Tailor
John Willis	40	Agricutural Labourer
Ruth Willis	40	Wife
Ann Willis	15	
Dorothy Willis	14	
Robert Willis	10	
Thomas Willis	4	
Mary Willis	2	
Ann Brown	60	Parishioner
Thomas Hallowell	62	Cartwright
William Hallowell	35	
Ann Hallowell	22	
John Hallowell	15	
Elizabeth Hallowell	13	

The above census and other lists were taken from early handwritten lists. The names and figures in some of the entries were not very clear, so some variation in spelling may have occurred.

Ellington Council – From Minute Book

1927	Office of overseer ceased to function.
1929	Rejection of Ellington Parish to Ashington u.b.c.
1934	Vote taken. 99% of population against so not to be proceeded with.
1937	Rateable value of Ellington Parish £8,369.
1947	Conference postponed owing to severe snowstorm.
1947	Mr. Abbott asks for permission to start a bus service from Ellington to Cresswell.
1948	Permission given for the bus service.
1948	Move to transfer from Morpeth Rural Council to Ashington U.B.C.

1948	Housing Act 1949 re bathrooms and washhouses to Council houses.
1950	Street Lighting, proposal first initiated in 1939, minimum lighting was provided by N.C.B.
1953	Coronation, number of children under 5 years – Linton 48, Ellington village 50, Ellington Colliery 23. Mugs to be given to the children. Also £12 to be divided between the three committees to be spent on the widows and spinsters over 60 and people over 65 years.
1953	As street lighting was to be turned over from the N.C.B. to N.E.E.B., the parish would have to pay; it having previously been free.
1956	Public lighting finally completed.
1957	New houses opposite Merten's Garage called Cheviot Close.
1958	Population of parish 1,264.
1962	Eight new houses built between Merten's garage and Cresswell Road, named Ravensworth Gardens.
1965-1970	Cresswell Road realigned.

Population Statistics from 1981 Census

	Total Pop:	0-4 yrs.	5-9	10-15	16-64	65-74	75-84	85+
Ellington	2428	215	192	198	1555	187	73	8
Cresswell	231	15	14	30	156	10	3	3
Lynemouth	2072	107	124	192	1312	246	80	13

Transport

With the coming of the Colliery to the village in 1910, a railway was needed to transport the coal. As it passed through Ashington it was not long before the local people saw it as a quick way of getting to town. The engine was called a "Tanky" and a coach was provided with wooden seats. As these were usually dirty, it was the habit to take along a newspaper to put on the seat before sitting down.

In the 1920-30's there were buses run by a number of proprietors, notably Seb. Johnson, Bowers, Britain, A. Wilkinson, and an Italian named Notrianni. Later Nesbit had a service to Ashington, and Mr. Batty had a service to Linton for many years. Mr. Abbot started a service to Cresswell in 1948. Hitherto it had been a Summer Only Service, starting in 1934.

In 1965 the Wansbeck Motor Company had a service from Ashington to Linton. Then finally all routes were taken over by the United Automobile Services.

Post Offices and Services

The following items up to 1925 are copied from Whites Directory:—
1897 The postal authorities put a driving post and a letter bag was left at Potland crossing. A messenger was despatched to deliver to Potland and Linton Colliery and Linton Tile Shed, North and South Linton, Hagg House and Highthorne.
1887 Whites Directory Lists J. Watson as Postmaster and Grocer in Ellington.
1901 Jane Finley, Post Office and Anthony Robson, Postman.
1925 Jane Finley was still officiating.

There was a sub Post Office in the second house on the left down the Ellington Bank and later in what is now the Bank Top Stores. This ceased before 1960, Mrs. M. Scott taking over from then and operating from her house in the Lynemouth Road.

Cresswell

There is no record of a Post Office until the 1930's.

Ellington and Cresswell Quarter Session 1594-1630

Elinore Peacocke of Ellington, Woodhorn Parish, did not attend church according to Statute (1593).
Jury of 1606. Henry Kirton of Cresswell – also on same charge – Morpeth Quarter Sessions.
Grand Jury, 1609. W. Brown of Cresswell, yeoman.
Grand Jury, 1611. Cuthbert Cresswell of Ellington.
Grand Jury, 1610. R. Humfrey of Cresswell, all presumably on same charge.
1616. Ralph Forster in Haghead Close, Ellington, murdered Thomas Swynhoe, a Justice of the Peace, with a sword worth 2/-.

Hexham Midsummer Session 1680

A swarm of bees belonging to Ephraim Cresswell of Cresswell went into the hive of W. Singleton.

Ellington and Cresswell Quarter Sessions 1687-1732

1687   John Richardson did scandalize and defame D. Blackburn and did call her a witch.
1705   Fraud with counterfeit watch.
1710   Unlicenced selling of fish.
1732   People of Cresswell pilfered and stole from castaways and wreck. Ship on rock, crew got ashore. Chest was found in the barn of J. Garret, who at first denied taking it, as did his servant J. Green. Both were fined £40 and £20 respectively. John Fisher was fined £20 for taking timber.

Ellington School (Reference also to Cresswell School)

The school was built in 1837, according to an inscribed stone bearing that date on the front of the building. However, some local people have said that the school was opened in 1836. Be that as it may, in 1976 it was closed when a new school was opened on the Highthorne Estate.

An earlier school may have existed, as White's Trades Directory lists a schoolmaster named William Athey. He could, of course, have been teaching elsewhere.

In 1847, William Adam was Headteacher, and prior to 1871 William Moffatt was in charge as a report in the "Morpeth Herald" states that an inspector visiting the school in December of that year gave the following report:—

"Very good in reading, not one of the children failing. Also good in other subjects. Mr. Moffatt is the teacher".

A Diocesan Inspector's report in May 1873 just says "Good results", but this contradicts an entry from the school Log Book, which is in the Public Record Office. It follows: "Week ending Nov 29th, 1873. Big boys who have entered school for the Winter, I find to be a long way back in their work, but hope by kindness and firmness to beget in them a love for school and study. Compulsory attendance very much required in Agricultural districts."

In May 1874, a new classroom was added also a large playground. Both were given by A. Baker-Cresswell.

An entry in the Log Book for 1875 shows a list of songs, "Wait for the Waggon", "Belle Mahone," "Listen Schoolmates," "Home Farm Yard", "Plough Boy", "Father's Return", "Keel Row", "Bonnie Pit Laddie", "Fisherman", "National Anthem".

April, Good weather in that year.

1876, Oct. Bad weather. Nov. Measles.

1877, Jan. School closed because of Fever and Measles.

1877, Feb. More Fever. Medical Officer visited Fishermans Row, Cresswell, complaints of bad sanitation, possible cause of Scarlet Fever.

1877, Still no law compelling children to attend school, as the Inspector's report well illustrates. Hopeless trying to teach anything other than Reading, Writing and Arithmetic, in such a school as this when half the children were off in the Winter owing to bad weather and a greater part of the Summer for haymaking and other farm work.

In 1879, Frank Wetheral took over as Headmaster and there was a more favourable report by the Inspector for religion.

An entry for 1880 states that school equipment was sent from Cresswell Infants' School to Ellington. The Cresswell School was built in 1838 by the Cresswell family. It had a small cottage built onto it for the teacher to live in. I have also seen it listed as a girls' school, but local people talk of their parents having attended the school, so it was probably for both sexes.

Kellys Directory for 1847 lists a Jane Wilson as a teacher and in 1858 Hannah Leech and Jane Murrey.

Whether the date of 1880 was when the school closed is not certain as I have been unable to find a firm date for its closure, or why two schools were built about the same time, as children from Cresswell were attending the one in Ellington built in 1837.

1893 This is a list of school poems:—

"Two little kittens", "The Beggar Man", "After Blenheim", "The Wreck of The Hesperous", "The lost minstrel".

1893 List of school songs:—

"When the rosy morn", "Beautiful May", "The Farmer's Boy", "Under the Willow", "Gathering Shells", "Old Xmas", "Wildwood Flower", "Lordly Gallant".

These lists of songs and poems changed periodically.

1893 The following is the Inspector's Report. It shows an improvement in the standard of education:—

"Reading, pretty accurate, but no modulation in voice. Standards 3 and 4 did not sufficiently understand what they read. Spelling and hand writing very fair".

"Composition fair. Written Arithmetic fair. Mental Arithmetic needs attention.

Teachers at Ellington School, 1924.
Backrow: Miss. Mitchell, Unknown, Unknown.
Middle row: Miss. Foster, Mrs. Fletcher, Miss. Friars, Miss. Kay.
Front row: Mrs. Bell, Mr. Rigby, Mr. Herron, Rev. Horsfall, Mrs. Elliot.

Photo: Courtesy of Mr. W. Barrons.

Poetry well known and fairly well understood. Grammar and Geography fair. Needlework very good."

The following entries show how much information can be abstracted from the Log Book. Such as weather, disease, shipwrecks and other events.

1890 Mar. 7. Hands hiring at Morpeth, many children away. School fee 1/- (5p). Mumps prevalent.

1891 March. Stormy weather. June, Whooping cough. Nov. Ship ashore at Quarry Point, many children away. Dec. Storm, no children from Linton as they could not cross the Lyne Burn owing to flooding.

1892 Feb. 19th. School closed owing to measles. Pupil teacher slapped Henry Marvin, cautioned never to strike a child again. Feb. 19th. Storma and heavy snow, only 11 children present. Mar. 19th Stormy. July 22nd. Whooping cough prevalent.

1904 Inspection report: Instruction is carried out mechanically and is little adapted to increase intelligence or have real educational value. November, No change, children show little interest in the monotonous work they have done and know hardly anything about it.

1906 Teaching careful but fails to secure efforts of scholars.

1906 Head Teacher – Davinia Urquarhart.

1910 Report: Teacher working hard but still scholars are not doing as well as they should.

1910 More children at school owing to building of colliery rows.

1913 Much improvement in school, children under control, good instruction. Effort seen in ready response and self effort of the children.

1914 Start of War. Dec. 10th Officer commanding the Scottish Horse, who were stationed at Cresswell Hall visited school to see about using it for giving lectures to the troops.

1915 Mar. 1st. Snow. Mar. 18th Fierce snow storm. July 2nd Whooping Cough. Oct. 6th Shropshire Yeomanry stationed at Ellington. Dec. 20th Measles.

1916 School closed for one week owing to measles. Mar. 1st very stormy, snow, rain. Mar. 23rd Snow again. Mar. 27th First fine day for weeks. April 3rd German airship over district. Most children out of bed all night to view. Nov. 3rd Bad storm. Nov. 27th Stormy. Dec. 20th Snow, temp 30°.

1917 This year was noted for its very severe weather. Feb. Severest frost for years. Snow fell as late as April 16th. Disease was prevalent, Scarlet Fever and Measles. June was very hot and in August children were off school with The Itch; the only time that it is recorded in the reports. This was also a very wet month. October saw the departure of Mr. Herron, the Headmaster, to take his part in the war of 1914–18. He joined the Naval Air Service. Mr. Richard took over as temporary Head.

1920 Report Children well behaved and responsive. Good progress in arithmetic and composition.

1926 Children will be transferred to new premises. Headmistress, Catherine Wilkie much praised.

The Ellington and Linton C. of E. School ceased to be recognised as a Public Elementary School. School closed on April 30th 1926. Ex-Army huts were used to house children until new schools at Lynemouth and Linton were opened. Only the original school was retained. This functioned as an infants' school until its closure in 1976, when the new school was opened on the Highthorne Estate.

List of School Masters/Mistresses

1847 William Adam
1870 William Moffatt
1879 Frank Wetheral
1903 George Herron
1926 Mrs. Fletcher
     Miss Manthorpe
1937 Miss Douglas
1947 Miss Davidson
1950 Mrs. McIntosh (Transferred to Highthorne new school)
1980 Mrs. Campbell

Snippets

1882 Mrs. Baker-Cresswell gave cloaks to the girls, it apparently being the annual custom.

1884 Two Cresswell parents complained of fisherfolk boys' behaviour to their girls on the way home from school, this being the second time that year. The boys were punished in the presence of the School Managers.

1884 Pupils absent for haymaking.

1887 Three boys withdrawn from school, family emigrating to America.

1890 No Cresswell children at school owing to sale of ship wrecked a few weeks' ago.

1893 John Foster was punished for striking Henry Greaves with a poker.

1902 Miss K. Jackson's salary as Headteacher was £65 a year.
1903 Cresswell children were warned about taking turnips from Farmer Chirney's field (Now Highthorne Estate).
1941 Bomb fell on Ellington Pit, shrapnel hit school.

Health

The Ellington School Log Book gave a daily report on the health of the pupils so I thought it would be of interest to produce the following list, as most of the diseases then prevalent are controlled by inoculation today.

Nov. 1876	Measles.
Jan. 1877	School closed, Scarlet Fever and Measles.
Feb. 1877	Scarlet Fever; Medical Officer visits Fisherman's Row, Cresswell, to inspect sanitary conditions of privies.
Jun. 1877	Whooping Cough.
Mar. 1879	Colds; Sore Throats.
Jan. 1880	Mumps, Scarlet Fever, School disinfected.
Apr. 1880	Still some cases of Scarlet Fever.
Feb. 1881	Measles.
Mar. 1881	School closed; Measles.
July 1882	Chicken Pox.
Nov. 1882	Sore Throats.
Jan. 1884	Whooping Cough.
Jan. 1888	Scarlet Fever.
Aug. 1890	Mumps.
Nov. 1890	Mumps, Colds, Sore Throats.
Nov. 1891	Mumps.
June 1891	Whooping Cough.
Feb. 1892	Measles, School closed.
July 1892	Whooping Cough.
July 1894	Measles.
1895-98	Measles prevalent.
1899	Whooping Cough.
1902	Measles; School closed.
Nov. 1902	Scarlet Fever.
May 1903	Scarlet Fever.
Nov. 1904	Whooping Cough.
Mar. 1905	Mumps, very prevalent.
Aug. 1906	Scarlet fever; first at Cresswell, then at Ellington.
Jan. 1907	Influenza (note: first mention of this complaint).
Mar. 1907	Diptheria at Cresswell; all children excluded from school.
June 1907	Diptheria; School closed for disinfecting.
Nov. 1907	Still Diptheria.
Dec. 1907	School closed for Diptheria.
Sept. 1911	Whooping Cough.
Sept. 1912	Scarlet Fever at Cresswell.
July 1914	Whooping Cough.
Jan. 1916	Measles; School closed for a week.
May 1917	Scarlet Fever, measles; 25 children off.
Aug. 1917	Scarlet Fever – 19 cases.

Weather

In recent years, any abnormal weather conditions, such as extreme cold and prolonged hot spells, have brought forth a number of theories for such conditions. This has prompted me to include a chapter on weather conditions over the last 100 years.

The Ellington School Log Book contains a daily entry by the Headmaster, Mr. F. Wetheral, and others on the state of the weather up to 1917. Later information is from personal memories.

I think that an examination of the list will lead one to the conclusion that no definite weather pattern has emerged.

Dec. 1873	Bad weather.
April 1875	Good weather.
July 1877	Very wet, late harvest.
Dec. 1877	Stormy.
1878	Wet, late harvest.
Nov. 1878	Stormy.
Dec. 13th 1878	Snow.
Nov. 21st 1879	Severe weather.
Dec. 17th 1880	Stormy.
Jan. 1881	Bad weather, roads impassable.
Mar. 7th 1881	Stormy weather.
Sept. 16th 1881	Very stormy; only 10 pupils present.
Dec. 2nd 1881	Stormy.
Apr. 1882	Very stormy.
Dec. 15th 1882	Stormy.
Mar. 9th 1883	Bad weather; very stormy.
Mar. 16th 1883	Stormy.
Aug. 1883	Very wet; late harvest.
Mar. 10th 1884	Very stormy.
Aug. 28th 1884	Stormy.
Jan. 1885	Stormy
May 10th 1885	Stormy.
Aug. 23rd 1885	Stormy.
Nov. 20th 1885	Stormy.
Dec. 11th 1885	Again stormy.
Jan. 1886	Stormy.
Mar. 5th 1886	Snow storm.
1887	Bad weather.
Mar. 16th 1888	Stormy.
Feb. 1890	Storm, no children from Cresswell.
Nov. 1890	Cold.
Mar. 1891	Floods; stormy month.
Dec. 11th 1891	Storm; no children from Linton, could not cross Lyne Burn.
Feb. 19th 1892	Storm, heavy snow; only 11 children present.
Mar. 18th 1892	Stormy.
Mar. 3rd 1893	Stormy; roads flooded.
Dec. 29th 1894	Gales.
Jan. 1st 1895	Snow storm.
Oct. 1895	Roads flooded.

Sept. 1896	Stormy.
Feb. 1899	Snow.
Dec. 5th 1899	Snowstorm.
Nov. 15th 1901	Stormy.
Dec 5th 1902	Very stormy.
Jan. 9th 1903	Stormy.
Feb. 1903	Stormy.
Dec. 1903	Snowstorm.
Feb. 19th 1904	Snowstorm, very heavy.
Nov. 22nd 1904	Snowstorm.
Dec. 1904	Flooding.
July 21st 1905	Very hot weather.
Jan. 1906	Severe weather.
Mar. 10th 1906	Very cold; snow.
Oct. 18th 1906	Severe storm.
Nov. 1906	Very stormy.
Feb. 28th 1908	Snow.
Jun. 1st 1908	Very hot.
Jul. 1908	Still hot.
Apr. 1909	Snow, cold.
July 1911	Very hot.
Feb. 2nd 1912	Heavy snow; only 9 children present.
June 3rd-28th 1912	Very wet.
Oct. 24th-31st 1912	Rain, storms.
Nov. 29th 1912	Very cold.
Jan. 16th 1913	Snow.
May 7th 1913	Roads flooded.
Dec. 4th 1913	Snow.
Apr. 1st 1914	Weather very fine.
June 8-9th 1914	Very stormy.
Mar. 1st 1915	Fierce storm.
Mar. 19th 1915	North-east wind, driving snow.
Mar. 3rd 1916	Very stormy, snow, rain.
Mar. 23rd 1916	First fine day for weeks after 27 consecutive days of rain, sleet or snow.
Nov. 3rd 1916	Bad snowstorm.
Nov. 27th 1916	Stormy.
Dec. 20th 1916	Snow, temp. 36°F.
Feb. 1st 1917	Very cold weather.
Feb. 5th 1917	Snowstorm.
Feb. 6th 1917	Very severe frost, keenest for years.
Mar. 5th 1917	Very cold, snow.
Apr. 2nd 1917	Snowstorm, bad for the whole of the week.
Apr. 16th 1917	More snow.
June 1917	Very hot.
Aug. 27th 1917	Very wet month.
Dec. 5th 1917	Very cold.
Dec. 17th 1917	Snowstorm. No more weather reports.

I can remember some very cold winters and hot summers during the 1920's. The Winter of 1939-40 saw much snow. Then there was the great freeze-up of 1946-47. Nothing really outstanding until 1963, when there was another big freeze-up. 1976 saw one of the hottest Summers on record. Heavy snow fell in 1978 and again in 1979. In 1981 snow fell in December, followed by very low temperatures in 1982, lowest recordings for a century, also the longest spell of continuous frost. In Newport, Shropshire, one of the lowest temperatures ever recorded in this country was 14.8°F. In March there was flooding in many parts of the country. By May the temperature was 70°F. August was one of the driest on record.

1982-83. The Winter was very mild but late April and May was very wet, April being the wettest since records were first kept. This was followed by a hot spell lasting from July until September. This was marred, however, by two countrywide gales in early September which did much damage to crops and property.

1984 was heralded in by terrific gales which swept throughout the country causing much destruction. This was followed by the driest Summer since 1976. Reservoirs in many parts of the country were completely dry and there were restrictions on the use of water. Northumberland, however, was not affected. Very heavy rainfall throughout November did redress the dry Summer.

Hagg Farm

The farm was owned by Lord Vernon until 1850, when it was purchased by Mr. Baker-Cresswell. In 1924, when the Cresswell Estate was sold it was bought for £8,500 by the Wood family who had been the tenants for over 300 years. The farm consisted of a house, four cottages and 360 acres of land. The names of the various fields can be seen in the catalogue of sale in 1850, the total acreage then being 410 acres.

CATALOGUE OF SALE FOR HAGG FARM – Tenant Jacob Wood – 1850
Tithe rent charge £58.2.1d.

Field	Acres
Clover	32
Lanceys Hill	42
Colorish	38
Lancey Hill Bottom	14
Water Gate Close	42
Tile Hill Close	50
Calf Close	2
Garden Close	3
Hope Field	32
Reed Side	28
Warren Head	13
Fairbairn Close	33
Long Flat	38
Orchard	24
High Dam	15
Low Dam	2
Messuage	1
Cottages at Ellington	0
Waste Lands enclosed	1
	410 acres

The Local Inventor

Mr. T. Mertens, who used to own the garage in Ellington, is an inventor and has erected in his garden the prototype of a transport system.

Lightweight carriages are supported and guided by sets of wheels from above and below which are trapped by a guideway to prevent derailment.

The wheels can be fitted with tyres to suit different load weights, from heavy duty to lightweight. The speed would be about 8mph, with higher speeds at a later stage of development.

The system would operate mainly in city centres to serve railway stations, hospitals and supermarkets, thus relieving congestion in these areas.

The Government and some foreign countries have shown interest in the invention. Several countries have prototypes of either monorail or overhead suspension systems, but none is quite the same as this one which is patented as the Merten Dual Rail. Mr. Mertens also has plans of another invention – a tidal operated system for the generation of electric power.

The Plough Inn

The inn was built in 1802 and there was a major rebuild in 1854. This date can be seen in Roman numerals on one of the chimneys. Other alterations were carried out in the early 1980's.

The Plough Inn, Ellington. From a postcard printed by F. Frith and photographed by Tugwell in 1955, reproduced by courtesy of the Birmingham Central Library. The negative is in the Frith collection of photographs now in the Library.

The inn was owned by the Baker-Cresswell family but was bought by Captain W. S. Sanderson prior to the sale of the estate in 1924. It was subsequently sold to Messrs. Vaux. The following list of licencees was taken from Trade Directories. The earliest entry is in the list below, but there is no record of whether he was the first licencee.

W. Hallowell	1828
Cath Gutherson	1847
John Marshall	1887
Mr. Ross between 1887 and 1901.	
Mr. Temple	1901
Thomas Woodrow	1925
Major Wilstead	1927
G. Clark	1929
Mr. Tiplady	mid 1930's
Mr. Robinson	1938
Mr. Armstrong	1954
Mr. J. Major	1974-

Ellington – Places of Interest

Most of the old property in Ellington is in the area around the Plough Inn which was built in 1802. There is only one shop now, a general dealers owned by Mr. and Mrs. Robson. Trade Directories show that there were more in the past (see general history). In recent years there was a small sweetshop but this closed in 1980. The big house next to the existing shop was once the "Sun Inn". And another large stone house with outbuildings further along the road to Alnwick was Ellington Farm House. Whilst a short distance along the opposite side is a brick building which was once the Institute, opened in 1908 by Lady Ravensworth. Returning and looking down what is known as The Bank, on the opposite side of the Plough can be seen the Ducket. Built of stone with semi-castellated top, this building housed the pigeons for the Cresswell Estate. The adjacent stone houses were once occupied by estate workers.

Next to Hubbs' Garage there are a number of houses built in the 1970's on the site of the vicarage.

The old school, built in 1837, and now housing the library, is opposite.

The garage was once owned by Mr. Mertens who built it in 1947. Bricks were in short supply after the war, so it was built of stone taken from two old condemned cottages down the Ellington Bank. Further along the road there are more houses, and the turning on the left leads to Cresswell.

The pond field has recently been landscaped and made into a wild life reserve which it is hoped will prove an attraction for waterfowl.

Along on the opposite side a narrow footpath next to the hedge indicates the line of the road before it was straightened in the 1960's.

At the end of this path is Windmill Hill Lane, but there is no trace of the windmill from which it derives its name. This lane forms the eastern boundary of the estate which has been built during the last ten years, and is on the site of what was once Ellington Farm. The Highthorne Estate takes its name from a nearby Farm. There are no shops as yet, but it has a school, built in 1976, to take the place of the old one in the village.

Ellington Institute of 1908.   *Photo: L.C. Leach.*

Ellington Colliery Institute.   *Photo: L.C. Leach.*

Ellington, The Ducket. Photo: L.C. Leach.

Ellington School. *Photo: L.C. Leach.*

Ellington Colliery. *Photo: L.C. Leach.*

One of the houses along the Lynemouth Road, owned by Mr. and Mrs. Scott, has a sub-post office which is always an important part of a village.

On the south-east side of Ellington is a very important part of the community – Ellington Colliery. This is the main source of employment in the area.

On the other side of the road there are three colliery rows and a small Council Estate, as well as the large Highthorne Estate.

Ellington Colliery

Ellington Colliery was originally owned by the Ashington Coal Co., and they also bought most of the local farms at the sale of the Cresswell Estate in 1924.

Three shafts were sunk between 1909 and 1913, No's 1 and 2 downcast shafts being 13ft. (3.96m) in diameter were equipped for the winding of men and materials. No. 3 shaft 15ft. (4.620m) in diameter was only used for emergency winding and pumping water from the mine. All the winding engines were steam operated and the coal was raised in 12 cwt. (610Kg) tubs in double decked cages.

In 1947 all the mines were nationalized under the title National Coal Board. Output continued as before, mainly from hand-filled longwall faces, with a small proportion provided by hand filling into tubs in pillar and stall panels.

The coal was transported by means of conveyors and endless rope haulages.

There was a considerable reserve of coal, so it was decided to embark on an extensive programme of modernisation to increase output.

The following list of improvements took place during the years up to 1956:—

1. The handling of output in 2¼ tonne capacity mine cars.
2. The re-equipping of No. 1 and No. 2 shafts with new headgears, cage loading equipment etc.
3. The provision of 600hp fully automatic Metro-Vick electric winders housed in new buildings at No. 1 and No. 2 shafts.
4. The provision of heapsteads and equipment of each shaft for the efficient handling of mine-cars and minerals.
5. The elimination of coal preparation at the colliery by the transport of run-of mine output to the Lynemouth Central Washery, a distance of 1½ miles.
6. The provision of new pithead baths to replace those built in 1927, which were then said to be the first in Europe, and a medical centre. Also on the list were lamprooms and planned maintenance premises.
7. The reorganisation of underground transport. Providing locomotive haulage and fully automatic loading stations, backed by adequate bunkerage.

This modernisation was carried out as well as a steady increase in output. Work was completed by 1956.

By 1971 there were 1,450 men working at the pit and they produced 5,500 tonnes of coal a day.

Again more modern machinery was introduced including the following:— the continuous miner, a tracked vehicle which scrapes off a thick layer of coal, then shoots it back along a conveyor to be collected by another vehicle. 1 tonne of coal is deposited at a time and another machine has arms which scoops up the coal and deposits it in a vehicle which is driven off to another conveyor and this in turn takes it on its 5 mile journey to the surface.

Another machine which is a chainsaw mounted on a crab-like vehicle, combines with other machinery to cut on three faces, putting a horizontal line along the base of the face and one down the centre, this machine is followed by a driller and this makes a path into which charges are inserted. The face is then blasted and the coal transported to the surface. The seam of coal is 14ft (4.27m) approx. thick and 360ft (109.728m) below the seabed, and a second seam is worked 40ft (12.20m) below the seam, a far cry from the days of pick and shovel.

By 1982 the Ellington Pit was drawing 85% of its output with the use of the Continuous 400hp Miner, and it now has 13 of these machines. As can be seen by the preceeding paragraphs, the colliery has long been a testing ground for new advanced technology. This being typified by the introduction of an even larger Continuous Miner of 420hp and a 340hp heli-miner, both being the first of their type in Europe. The heli-miner is operated by seven men each shift and can produce more coal in a week than the total output of some smaller thin seam mines.

Five high speed 300hp locomotives are used to take the men to their work place.

Ellington is linked to the nearby Lynemouth pit to form the world's largest undersea mining complex and their joint annual output is around 2.2 million tonnes.

The miners of Ellington can be proud of their coal production as they were the first in the north-east and the third colliery in the country to draw 1 million tonnes in the financial year, 1982-83.

The present work force is around 2,170 men who produce approximately 45,000 tonnes of coal per week.

The highest weekly figure for production by one team of 20 men is 4,694 tonnes. They advanced 350m through thick coal in the Bass Shill seam 8 kilometres under the sea.

Investment has not only been made in machine technology but some £3 Million has been spent on new offices and ancillary buildings, such as new pithead baths, replacing those built in 1956, and new stables for the 50 ponies which are still used to transport materials. Another building has a control room which operates the main underground conveyor system. The same control room also operates the main pumping system in areas where there are water problems.

Two electric winders take 16 men per cage underground from the surface and recently installed is an Otis lift operated by automatic control and is said to be the first to be installed in a mine in Europe. There is also a saving in manpower as the winderman, banksman and onsetter are not needed.

Pit Rules 1912

Cavilling rules and prices for Betty Pit, 1912.

Putters standing rank up to 130yds (118.95m) ¼d per score, for every additional 30yds (27.45m) 1.¼d per score extra. The rank to be measured from the middle of the flat and to the two nearest hand and two furthest off places to be taken for measurement. The rank to be measured fortnightly, but any places where the putting is done by the shift are not to be taken into account in the rank measurement. Putters at shiftwork and taken to put during the shift, to be paid by arrangement with the Overman ¼, ½ or ¾ shift, according to the overtime worked, at the rate of 3/2d per shift. Putter Hewers, special Putters and spare putters to be paid average score price of the pit.

Trapping to be paid for each door   3d per shift
Leading timber and plates in   2d per score

Casting timber at flat	3d per load
Long led tubs over 30yds (27.45m)	1/- per fortnight
If long led tubs for odd days only, 1d per shift to be paid.	
Wet putting in Whole places	1d per score extra
Wet putting in Longwall coal filling	3d per shift extra
Training ponies for 1st fortnight	1/- per day
Training ponies for 2nd fortnight	6d per day
Training ponies for 3rd fortnight	3d per day
Going with tub	6d per shift

When it is an advantage to go part way with two tubs, to be paid ½. Going with one in cases where men are far apart, 3d per shift in coal filling flats where it is necessary (for the purpose of putting the coals of fillers who are squaring up) for them to go back to a flat at which they have been previously putting during the same shift. This does not apply to putters who only change once from one flat to another during the shift.

Lying Money: Should the putters be stopped by reason of the pits standing for want of wagons they will be paid "Lying Money" after the first half hour, at the rate of 6d per hour. They will however be expected to lead in timber, or do other work in the time, should the Overman desire them to do so. No compensation will be paid for loss of time caused by an accident in the pit, or other cause than as stated. But in the case of a stoppage caused by a fall of roof, accident to engine, sets, or similar causes when the putters, on being requested have rendered assistance, they will be paid the same rate as for "Lying Money".

The Colliery Rows

The colliery houses were built around 1909-10, thus bringing a new community into what had been a rural village. There are three rows, although I doubt whether there are many miners of working age living there today. Certainly not the under-manager, overman, master-shifter, engineer, foreman joiner, etc. who lived in the First Row in the early days of the industry. Indeed, some of the titles no longer exist or have been changed.

Mrs. Cowton, who lived in the Second Row, had a small shop in the back yard which catered for the daily needs of the members of the community. Later, she had her shop outside a bungalow opposite the rows. Mrs. Taylor also had a shop in the rows.

There were some very large families – from seven to thirteen children in a family. This was no doubt the reason for extending the village school by the introduction of some ex-army huts in 1924.

Also, having a growing population, it was possible to form a choir for Cresswell Church. Mr. Alf Cowton was organist and choir master. Also in the choir were Mr. Stan Cowton – tenor, Edith Jacques – contralto, and Mr. Jack Scott – tenor. An orchestra was formed in the 1920's at the instigation of Mr. R. Tait who played the cello and bass fiddle.

Linton

There is evidence for a Linton Mill dating to 1307. It stood near the present dwelling which bears the same name. Linton was part of the parish of Widdrington until 1888 when it merged with Ellington.

The Colliery:

Borings for coal took place in the 1840's, but it was not until 1895 that a shaft was sunk by the Ashington Coal Co. The colliery also had its own brick works and a rail link to Ellington and Ashington.

With the closure of the mine in 1969 what had been a thriving community had to face many changes. Some miners transferred to other local pits, whilst others moved to the Midlands to work in the mines there.

The Community:

The Ashington Coal Co. proceeded to establish colliery rows and a school, as had been the practice in other mining areas. The school was not very substantial, having only a corrugated iron roof, but it lasted until 1925 when it was replaced by the present one.

The first school was run by the Church of England and its headmaster was Mr. Harrison who transferred from Ellington School.

School life was very different from today. Discipline was strict and truancy was severely dealt with as the following incident, told by Mr. G. Horn, illustrates:

Once a week, pedalling over from Morpeth would come the tall gaunt figure of the School Board Man whose job it was to check up on any absentees from school. One fine day young Chris Wood decided that the joys of the countryside would be better than a stuffy classroom. Unfortunately, he chose the same day that the School Board Man arrived. The teacher had to report his absence, so away sped the upholder of authority first to the lad's home then to the field with the burn running through it. It was not long before the School Board Man could be seen pedalling towards the school with one hand on the handle-bar and the other firmly grasping the ear of the truant who had to jog along to keep up with the bicycle. No doubt it was some time before someone else decided to miss school.

In those days children left school at the age of 14, except if they won a scholarship to a Secondary School where the leaving age was 16 years. The talented pupil, however, was not sure of a place as many families were too poor to pay for the school uniforms and books that were required.

On leaving school most of the lads would go to the pit and the girls "to place" (domestic service). There was very little else for them to do. So, with their trunks containing clothes and personal items, they would depart for Morpeth or the surrounding farms.

Very often their destination would be decided at the "Hiring" days, which were held in Morpeth and elsewhere. Here, farmers and others would state terms for the employment of farmhands and domestic servants.

In 1904, a hall similar in construction to the school was built. Many functions were held there and the Methodists held services there. The Church of England held their services in the old school, but later shared with the other denomination an arrangement which still exists in the new church of St. Aidan which was consecrated in 1965.

The Co-operative store was opened in 1925 and served the village until its closure in 1971. Today there is only one shop serving the community.

Very little industry has come to the village, although some of the ancillary buildings in the redundant mining complex are being used by three small businesses, an air filter manufacturer, a dealer in motor spare parts, and a firm repairing earth moving vehicles and machinery.

Social Activities:

The Institute was opened in 1925-26 and was the centre for much of the social life. A Literary Society was formed in the late 1920's and a branch of the Women's Institute held meetings there in 1930.

There were film shows and the Horticultural Society also held shows there.

J. Geir produced "Snow White" in the early 1920's and in 1936 the Welfare Players staged their first production, consisting of three short plays. One was "A dose of Physic". Mr. Len Morris played the lead, supported by Mrs. L. Morris, Miss Wrigglesworth, Miss A. Ainsley, Mr. T. Straughan and Mr. W. S. Wood. The second play was "In safe custody". Mrs. W. Dixon took the lead part, others were Mr. W. S. Wood, Miss J. Chester, Mrs. E. Harrison, Mrs. E. Wrigglesworth and Mr. L. Morris. The third play was "At the sign of the Bluebell". The lead was taken by Miss E. Ainsley, also appearing were Mr. W. S. Wood, Miss N. Jacques, Mr. T. Straughan and Mrs. L. Morris.

During the war years, there were many Ensa concerts, but today they are no local choral or dramatic societies.

Sport:

A cricket club was formed in 1926, captained by W. Hallowell. He lived in Ellington so perhaps this explains why there is no mention of a cricket club in that village. By 1930 they had teams in both A and B Leagues and in the East Northumberland Schools League. In 1935 they won the Alnwick and District League Cup. They played until the outbreak of War, when the call up stopped most sporting activities. There has not been a revival since.

Football too played a prominent part in the life of the village. In 1926 there was a team in the Coquetdale League and in 1930 they had a team in the Ashington Welfare League. In 1934 they won the Morpeth Cottage Hospital Cup and in the same year were champions of the Coquetdale League. Today there is a team called Linton and Woodhorn in the Sunday League. In 1936, Linton Institute were in the Billiards League but the game has long since fallen out of favour and has not been replaced by Snooker as has happened elsewhere, but by the game of Pool.

Tennis and Badminton were popular before the war. Today there is a Women's Bowls Club which has been quite successful, and the local Darts Team plays in the Stobswood League.

Linton Societies:

Linton Colliery Welfare Institute
Women's Institute
Mothers' Club
Social Club
Junior Football Club
Horticultural Society

Lynemouth

The spelling of the name Lynemouth has changed from that recorded in early documents, because it was once spelt Linmouth, and Linemouth. The name was taken from the small estuary or burn which was described as a pretty brook rising west of Espley.

The earliest reference to Lynemouth is in 1240, when it was given to John, a son of Robert Rue, together with Hurst, as a reward for military service, but precisely what this meant is not recorded.

The next record is of a Sir Ralph de Eure who died in the reign of Henry V owning land there. He also owned land in Haydon and Ellington.

In 1663, William Horsley was assessed for county rates there, and in 1721 Dr. Watson left an estate in the village to his daughter. Land was also held by Mr. Bradford in 1832. However, the principle landowner in the early 19th Century was Mr. Atkinson who owned some 315 acres, of which one farm was let to a tenant farmer.

The following are the names of fields, taken from a map of 1832: West Linmouth, Dike Close, Sharretts, East Sharretts, North Linefield and Linefield.

The village was in the parish of Woodhorn, and in 1801 only 12 people lived there. This figure had doubled by 1811, and by 1921 there were still only four houses and 22 people. Before passing on to the later history of the village, mention should be made of Dene House, which was built before 1760. It was owned by the Cresswells in the early part of this century and tenanted for many years by the Stamp family. It is now occupied by a scrap metal dealer who has recently renovated the property. The house is situated near the river between Lynemouth and Ellington.

In 1923 the Ashington Coal Co., having acquired most of the land, built a new township. And by 1926 there were over 500 houses, some shops, and a population of 2,000. A railway line was built from the pit at Ellington, passing through Lynemouth on its way to Ashington, with later connections to the Lynemouth colliery opened in 1934, but by 1984 it was being run down as most of the coal seams were approached from Ellington.

A halt was provided near where the present footbridge is situated. Like the travellers from Ellington, the locals would have to take their newspapers to put on the dirty seats of the carriages which were pulled by the Tanky. The railway ran parallel to the road and effectively cut the village in half. The road was also realigned between the two villages. Originally, it was no more than a track which can still be followed near Dene House and along the back of the Social Club, and coming out by the colliery rows at Ellington.

The Church of St. Aidan was dedicated in 1925 and at that time the chancel could be screened off to allow the rest of the building to be used for dances and other functions. At a later date panelling, pews and an organ were installed. A hall was also built and the Catholic Community was allowed the use of it for the celebration of Mass.

The Methodists had various meeting places until 1927 when a hall was built. The foundation stone was laid by Lord and Lady Runciman (as reported in the Morpeth Herald. There is no stone bearing an inscription to be seen, and a board with various dates only mentions Lady Runciman.

Trademen in the 1920's and early 1930's:

Albion Terrace: Crisp, Newsagent and General Dealer. Dewhirst, Chemist and Barber. Graham, General Dealer and Pork Butcher. Easton, Newsagent, Hardware, etc. Clavering, Post Office and General Dealer. Wilkinson, Newsagent, and General Dealer. Foster, Boots and Shoes. He was also a cobbler.

The church of St. Aidan, Lynemouth.   *Photo: L.C. Leach.*

Lynemouth School.   *Photo: L.C. Leach.*

Lynemouth Institute. Photo: *L.C. Leach.*

Market Square: There was a hairdresser. Smails, Butcher, and the Co-op are the only two businesses to remain in continuous occupation to this day. Other shops have changed owners many times over the years. Elliot, Bakers. Bardon, Ice Cream and Sweets. Pearson, Grocer. Moyes, Fish and Chips.

The Lynemouth Inn was opened in 1925 and the school in 1926, it was augmented by five ex-army huts and had a staff of 14. Mr. Herron was the Headmaster, and had previously been at Ellington School for 22 years. He was transferred to Lynemouth when the Ellington school closed in 1926. But the school at Ellington continued as an infants' school, and older children were transferred to the new school or elsewhere. Mr. Herron retired in 1940. Other headteachers were:— Mr. Graham – 1940-1967, Mr. Perris – 1967-1981, Mrs. Hall – 1981-1984, Mr. Rodgers – 1984-.

The Council was formed in 1918, but it was not until 1925 that there were elected councillors.

The next major building took place around 1939 when council houses were built between Park Road and the railway. A new Post Office was opened in Albion Terrace but unfortunately it was destroyed by a bomb in the war of 1939-1945. One person was killed (Mrs. Athey) and many more were injured. After the war a sub-post office was opened in one of the shops and more council houses were built. More council houses were also built in Dalton Avenue and Market Square. In 1938, a foundation stone was laid for Aged Miners' Homes.

During the 1960's, the Alcan Smelter came into being, providing many jobs for local people, as well as using coal from the nearby pits. Many of the National Coal Board farms are leased to Alcan, some of which are used for grazing cattle and others for the growing of cereals.

Bomb damage, 1939-45 war, Lynemouth.

Social Activities

As with all communities, the social life developed with the growth of the population.

The Welfare Hall and Institute was opened in 1925 and visited by the Duke of York in 1928. One of the first functions to be held in the hall was an horticultural show, an event which is still held to this day. Leek shows were held from 1929 and are still very popular. With the establishment of the film industry, cinemas were opened throughout the country and in 1927 a cinema was opened in the Welfare Hall in spite of objections from the Ashington cinema owners.

The Institute has been redecorated several times. On one occasion in the 1950's Mr. J. Mackenzie painted a set of murals. On the wall of the entrance lobby there is a crest of a lion rampant with Latin inscription 'E. Tenebris Lux' (Out of darkness into light). On the left hand side of the entrance hall there is a scene of a castle. A man on horseback has a raised sword. The right hand mural depicts three figures practising archery. They are beside a river with a castle in the background. The wall next to the stairs which leads to the upper floor has a scene of a jousting tournament, with knights charging and many spectators, a castle and marquees. All the murals are of the medieval period.

The building was extensively modernised in 1983. The Lynemouth Choral Society was formed in 1926 by Mr. Jack Bolsdon who was also the conductor. The venue for the first concert was the new Hall and the soloists were Miss K. Fornear and Miss May Walsh.

By 1935 it had developed into the Lynemouth Operatic Society and the first production under its new name was "H.M.S. Pinafore", with the same conductor. Mr. Edwin Harrison was the stage manager. The society flourished until 1939 when the war halted its activities. The final production was "The Yeoman of the Guard". There was a lapse of over 20 years before a Choral Society was formed by Mr. Alf Cowton who died in 1973. He was also organist at the church. The main singers were Stan Cowton, tenor, Matt Turnball, Mollie Hunt, H. Robinson, and Alice Moffat, piano. Songs from the operas, including Carmen and Maritana, were rendered at one concert.

After the death of Mr. A. Cowton, the society once again ceased its activities.

The British Legion formed a Women's Section in 1925 and in 1926 a Women's Co-operative Society was founded. The Labour Party has always been well represented in Lynemouth. Nevertheless, in 1928 a Liberal Association was formed and it has been a recent success with the election of a councillor.

In 1930, a branch of the Royal and Ancient Order of Buffaloes was founded and in the same year the Unionists Association (Wansbeck Division) formed a branch for women. The Girl Guides started a troop in 1931, and in the same year the Lynemouth Primitive Methodist Church formed a Good Templar Lodge.

The Institute was acquired by the Miners from the Ashington Coal Company in 1934.

There was a Burns Society in 1935, but it no longer exists. Lynemouth's first doctor, Dr. Skene was a founder member.

Sport

Sport always plays a big part in any community and Lynemouth is no exception.

There was a cricket club in 1925 and by 1930 it boasted two teams in the Alnwick and District League. These teams were playing until the outbreak of the war and for a number of years after. There has been talk of a revival but so far this has not taken place.

Football was perhaps the main local sport and there was certainly a local team by 1930. It was in the Ashington Welfare League and still is. There was a junior team and St. Aidans Church had a team in 1936. Today the Lynemouth Inn has a team in the Morpeth Sunday League, and Alcan (Lynemouth) play in the Tyneside Amateur League.

It must be remembered that teams were drawn mainly from pitmen and, being a reserved occupation, they were not required to serve in the armed forces, so had a continuity of members denied to those outside the mining areas. This, however, does not explain why the cricket should have lapsed.

Boxing, during the 1930's was represented by the O'Keefe family; six brothers were boxing about the same time. The Lister brothers were also boxing at that time and Harry Lister fought Jack London in 1939.

By 1935 there were Table Tennis Teams in the A and B division of the Ashington Colliery Welfare League, as well as Tennis and Badminton Teams.

The Sea View Cycling Club also had Lynemouth members.

Darts was also popular then and is even more so today.

Most Social Clubs and local Inns have both male and female teams, Lynemouth being no exception.

Lynemouth is also represented in the Broomhill and District Domino League.

The game of quoits, once a popular game, is not played as much today.

Of recent years, a bowling club has been formed.

The game of Billiards was popular before the war, but this has been replaced by snooker, T.V. coverage of championship contests no doubt being the reason. There are two teams in the Drybrough's Blyth and District Snooker League.

Pool is also played in many clubs and pubs.

Whippet Racing used to play a prominent part in the life of the pitman in pre-war days. Races are still held, but equally popular are greyhounds.

Golf also has many adherents in the local villages.

Pigeon Racing continues to be popular.

List of Societies in Lynemouth:

Miners Welfare, also Junior Section.
Co-operative Women's Guild
Church Senior and Junior Club
Church Fellowship
Townswomen's Guild
Mothers' Union
1st Scout Troup
Brownies
Pre-School Play Group
Horticultural Society
Leek Club
Ex-Servicemen's Association
Lynemouth Citizens Association Group

Vicars and Ministers of St. Aidans, Lynemouth

1925   F. S. Moore
1929   F. C. Westgarth
—   H. H. Bean
1941   J. J. Lapping
1947   P. W. Rudge
1953   J. E. Linton
1959   A. C. Beniams was the first vicar of Lynemouth when it became a parish in 1961. Prior to that date it was a Conventional District under the parish of Woodhorn and its incumbents were Ministers.
1963   J. W. Dowling
1982   B. Skelton

Preston Tower

Robert Harbottle built the Tower around 1392, and it originally consisted of a long building with towers at each corner. Half of it was demolished after the union with Scotland in 1603, when there was no longer any need for the many fortified towers which had been built throughout the country.

As previously stated the Tower came into the possession of the Baker-Cresswell family in 1861, and in 1864 Henry Robert, who was living in the nearby mansion, initiated various improvements to the Tower. The north side had a new wall built onto it and some cottages attached to the side were removed.

In a second-floor room a large clock was installed, the face of which occupies one of the windows.

The striking mechanism is the "flat bed type" invented by Lord Grimthorpe and first used for Big Ben in 1860. The bell was cast in Newcastle.

Tanks were also installed. These were filled with spring water pumped into them. The water served the nearby house and farm. The Tower is well worth a visit as it gives some idea of the grim living conditions prevailing in those times. There are maps, ballads and stories displayed. There is also a model showing what the Tower originally looked like.

The gardens contain a number of interesting trees and shrubs. Visiting hours are 10am-6pm daily, April-September.

Preston Tower.   *Courtesy of Major T.H. Baker-Cresswell.*

Woodhorn

The parish of Woodhorn was bounded on the north by the Chapelry of Widdrington, on the south by Bedlingtonshire, on the east by the North Sea, and on the west by Bothal and Ulgham.

It comprised of the chapelry of Newbiggin and the townships of Cresswell, Ellington, Hurst, Linmouth, North Seaton, Woodhorn and Woodhorn Demesne.

In 1881 Cresswell and Ellington were combined to make a separate parish for all ecclesiastical purposes.

The following shows the population of the townships within the old parish, excluding the Chapelry of Newbiggin:—

	1801	1811	Houses	Families	1821 persons	Annual Value £
Cresswell	183	191	46	51	303	1,863
Ellington	213	114	51	51	255	3,369
Hurst Nth.	50	44	9	9	42	682
Linmouth	12	24	4	4	22	330
Seaton Nth.	182	150	32	34	159	2,116
Woodhorn	143	136	31	31	155	1,703
Woodhorn Demesne	10	14	2	2	8	936

Woodhorn as it is today is comprised of a few cottages, but most of the labour for the colliery which was opened in 1887 came from elsewhere. The pit closed in 1981 and is now an industrial archaeological site. Woodhorn Farm, which stood opposite the road to Newbiggin, was demolished in the 1970's, and a fixed steam engine which was found intact in one of the outhouses was taken to Beamish museum.

The principal occupant of the farm was Jacob Watson who resided there in 1855. In 1857 he invented a reaping machine and in 1865 he had a set of paired steam engines constructed for ploughing. This was the second set in all the country. For other farming improvements he was given a knighthood in 1889.

There a sailless windmill nearby where the farm used to stand, and also the Milhouse which has recently been renovated.

Woodhorn Demesne was a small area opposite the church. The Baker-Cresswells had a mansion there known as the Red House, but there is no trace of it now (see Cresswell).

Church of St. Mary

The Church of St. Mary was the parish church and was used by the surrounding villages until the building of the church of St. Bartholomew in 1836 at Cresswell.

The church has its origins in the Saxon period when it consisted of a chancel, aisleless nave, and a tower. Traces of the typical "long and short work" can be seen in the base of the tower. More evidence came to light in 1882 when a trial excavation near the altar indicated by dowsing revealed Saxon footings.

Two simple round-headed windows are dated to the 11th century. The Normans added north and south aisles. There are also examples of Early English Architecture dating to the 13th and 14th Centuries, and the great chancel arch is 13th Century. No further alterations or additions seem to have been carried out until 1884, when there was extensive restoration. There were major repairs to the fabric in 1975-1976.

The Church of St. Mary, Woodhorn.   *Photo: L.C. Leach.*

The Church of St. Mary, Woodhorn.   *Photo: L.C. Leach.*

The church is now a museum and cultural centre administered by the Leisure and Publicity Department of the Wansbeck District Council, who arrange travelling exhibitions. On permanent display there are examples of carved stones, 16 of which are associated with the church, whilst others are from the keep in Newcastle and elsewhere.

The most outstanding of the Woodhorn Collection are the fragments of Saxon cross. There are four pre Norman upright grave markers and some grave slabs of medieval date. Pride of place must be the effigy which is said to be of Agnes de Valence, wife of Hugh Balliol the brother of Edward Balliol, King of Scotland.

A book giving details of the above is obtainable at the museum.

There are other items on permanent display, as well as memorials to the Baker-Cresswells, Watsons, and others.

Church Wardens Accounts

Rates for Woodhorn Parish 1732:
Woodhorn – £1.9.3d. Mill – 2/10d. Hurst – 9/4d. Lynemouth – 5/10d. North Seaton – £1.7.3d. Ellington – £1.9.3d. Mill – 2/2d. Cresswell – 17/6d.

Churchwarden's Account – Ellington Tithes to Woodhorn 1893.

Mr. Ely Wood, Hagg House	£6.4.0d.
Mrs. Cresswell, High Moor	£3.1.0d.
Mr. Cresswell, East Moor	£1.0.4d.
Mr. Chierney, Ellington Farm	£35.18.6d.
Mr. Cresswell, MIll Farm	£1.5.2d.

Tithe Payment of 1842

Ellington in the parish of Woodhorn – amounts payable to Tithe Owners.

Vicar of Woodhorn	£46.9.3d.	Value in Bushels
Rev. Cook	£121.16.0d.	Wheat 7½
Adam Askew	£121.16.0d.	Barley 3/10½
		2/9

Hagg Farm

Owner: Lord Vernon. Tenant: John and Jacob Wood.
410 acres, payable to previous three people: £6.4.1d., £25.9.0d., £25.09.0d.

Owner A. Askew				
Dene House	T. Bell	573 acres		
High Thorne	Woods	327 acres		
Owner Baker-Cresswell				£39
West Moor	T. Bell, J. Willis		£18.16.9d.	
East Moor	T. Bell	303 acres	£18.16.9d.	
Owner A. Askew		16 acres		
Owner Baker Cresswell				
Ellington Farm	195 acres	£1.4.1d.	£15.10.4d.	
Woodlands	2 acres		£15.10.4d.	
Tenant: John Purvis				
Margaret Purvis,	garden in village	2 acres	£1.10.0d.£1	£1

Tithe Payment of 1848

The Baker-Cresswell Estate, including Bog Hall – 1,000 acres.

420 acres of Arable Land.

497 acres Meadow and Pasture Land.

148 acres Woodland.

2 acres Roads.

350 acres of enclosed land.

Wasteland and quarries 90 acres protected from tithes other than corn on payment of £1.2.8d.

Blakemoor Farm, Mrs. E. Cook 340 acres protected from tithes on hay on payment of 3/4d per year.

Township lands not otherwise exempted from payment of tithes, there is a due to the Vicar by every person who has fewer than five calves from Easter-Easter. 1½d. for every new calved cow and 1d for every barren one instead of calves and milk.

Worshipful the Wardens and Community of Mercers of London and the incumbent Curate for the time being of St. John's Chapel in Middlesex are entitled to tithes of corn and grain, in equal parts. Instead of tithes the sum of £102.4.4d. can be paid to St. Johns. Also the sum of £40.12.6d. rent charged to the local Vicar instead of other tithes.

T. Muckle of Bog Hall payable in lieu of tithes the sum of £142.16.10d.

To the Vicar of Woodhorn £40.12.6d., and to the Warden Mercers etc. £51.2.2d. St. John's Chapel £51.2.2d.

John Baker-Cresswell's Farm £733.3.3d. To the Vicar of Woodhorn £33.2.6d. Mercers Co. £25.15.0d. St. John's £25.15.0d.

Mr. Cook of Blakemoor Farm £345. To the Vicar of Woodhorn £7.10.0d. Mercers Co. £25.6.9d. St. John's £25.6.9d.

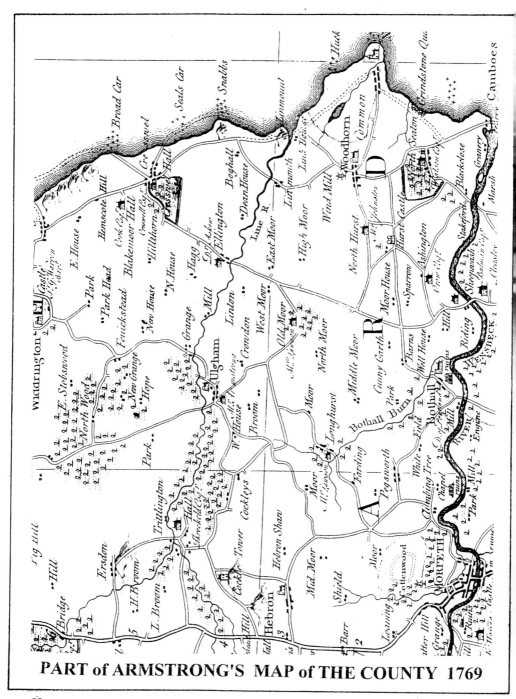

PART of ARMSTRONG'S MAP of THE COUNTY 1769

PART of GREENWOOD'S MAP of THE COUNTY 1828

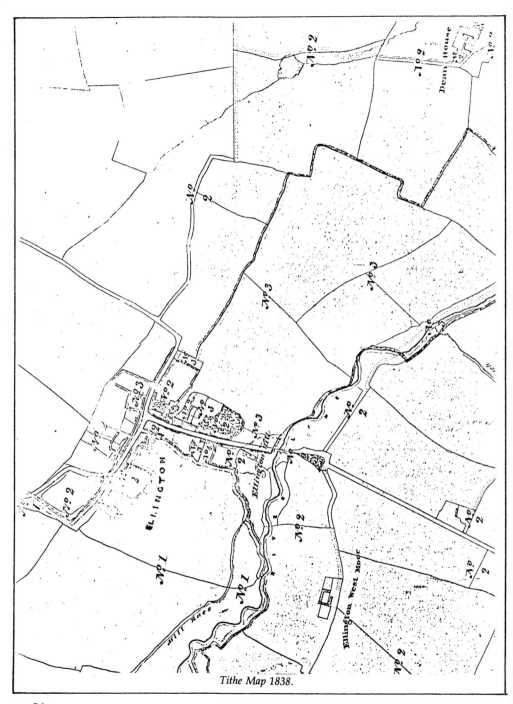

Tithe Map 1838.

94

The Old Ballad of Cresswell Tower

Of Cresswell in old Northumberland
A doleful song I sing
And of a tower which there doth stand
And stood when John was King.

Once in that tower a lady dwelt
As gentle and as fair,
As any to whom brave knight e'er knelt
In England or anywhere.
And brothers three the lady had
Who loved their sisters dear
But one thing made those brethren sad
To lose her they oft would fear.
For Denmark's stoutest and noblest knight
Of royal pedigree
Had seen that maid and her troth to plight
Determined was he.

One day that lady was in her tower.
The wind roared high in squalls.
She rose and watched from the topmost tower
And quailed at the Cresswell calls.

She knew that Rollo was on the sea
Coming his love to meet
And shame it were that ready was she
That faithful heart to greet.
And now his coble had neared the shore
And was bounding over the wave,
The spray dashed high from each quivering oar
"Oh God, that coble save!"
That prayer was heard, he rode the land
But oh what a sight is there
Three stalwart forms stalk over the sand
And murder is in the air,
For armed with battleaxe and sword
Marched on those brethren three;
And above the storm her doom she heard:
"That meeting must not be,"
"Not be," spake out that royal Dane,
"Not be" those Cresswells cried.
"Lay on then" spoke he back again,
"Lay on" the three replied.

The blows fell fast and furious then
But the odds were one to three,
The brothers were stout Northumbrian men,
Each well nigh stark as he.

The lady looked down from the old Pele Tower,
And saw her lover was slain,
And never after that dreadful hour
Would her lips touch food again,
And ever since in white array
At midnight's awful hour
A graceful and pale and beautiful maid
Walks round that old Pele Tower.
And ever as those weird Cresswell calls
Bid mariners to beware,
A treble chord from the ruined walls
Is the moan of that lady fair.

Folk Tale – The Cresswell Tailor

Once there lived at Cresswell a tailor whose greatest infirmity was a fondness for a strong drink. This weakness led him into many a scrape, for although when he was sober he was friendly and even timid, after a night's tippling he became arrogant and insolent. He boasted of his skill, declaring that no tailor in Northumberland could match him at his trade, and forced himself upon unwilling listeners.

He was in this mood one evening in the little inn at Cresswell. It was a dark night, dark outside and dark inside, for there was no moon, and the room was lit only by a little lamp that left the corners in half-darkness.

Two or three men were seated on the bench listening to the tailor, and another, a stranger in a three-cornered hat, sat by himself in one of the dim corners. The tailor was on his feet in the middle of the floor, holding his mug in one hand, and waving the other about as he declaimed to his little audience.

"Someone mentioned coats," he cried. "Coats! Why, there is not a tailor between Tweed and Tees that can make a coat with less cloth than me. I can make a coat that will fit any man's pocket and figure, that will suit and fit him, as never before. I can make a coat for any man, prince or pauper. Ay, I could make a coat for the devil himself, if he were here".

The men nodded approvingly, but the stranger in the corner kept silent. His silence maddened the tailor, for in this mood he demanded agreement. Putting down his mug, he advanced closer to the stranger, crying, "Did I see you shake your head, sir?" But the stranger still kept quiet.

"You did shake your head sir!" the tailor went on. You imply that I am boasting eh? Come here and let me see the face of the man who dare shake his head at the tailor of Cresswell. I don't like quiet men who sit sulking in dark corners. Come out and let me see the colour of you".

Still the stranger did not move. "He refuses!" cried the drunken man. "He refuses! Well, I'll show him what happens to the man who insults me." And he plunged forward to strike the stranger. But he had not noticed a little stool which stood between him and the corner. Bang went his toes on the stool and he pitched forward, striking his nose on the corner of the bench, and making the blood spurt. For a minute the house was in an uproar, one man holding the tailor down, another pushing a huge key down his back, another calling for help as vociferously as if the house were on fire. In the hurly-burly the stranger took his leave.

It was midnight before the tailor left the inn, for, when his nose had stopped bleeding, he began to look upon the escape as a victory for him, a triumph to be celebrated. But no story can be told over and over for ever, and at last he was turned out to make his way home. He set off drunkenly along the dark lane, but he had not gone far before he saw in front of him the stranger in the three-cornered hat. Inside the inn, in the presence of cronies, he had felt valiant, but now that he was alone and cold his valour began to leave him.

"You said, tailor, that you could make a coat to suit anyone, even the devil himself, didn't you?" said the stranger. "I did," faltered the tailor. "Well," replied the other, sinisterly, "I'm your man, I give you 'till a week to-night to make a coat. Please me, and I will know that you are as good as your word, and you will be paid well. But if the coat does not please me, beware for I will have you, every inch, body and soul. Now measure me."

With his heart knocking at his ribs, the tailor took out his tape. He never knew how he managed to finish the measuring. He only knew that when he had done and the devil had vanished he looked at his tape and found it singed, and his finger-tips were stinging as if they had been burnt.

He spent a troubled and sleepless night and when he arose the next morning he faced a scolding wife. "Is it not enough for you to waste the evening squandering what little money we have on drink?" she cried, "Must you also spend the night tossing and turning and keeping others from their sleep"?

"Ah wife," replied the husband, "if your conscience was as troubled as mine, you would not be able to sleep" and then he told her of his meeting with the devil.

His wife had no sooner heard the story than she ran out sobbing to seek consolation from her neighbours, and she was so loud in her grief that half the women in the village came running to hear of her trouble. In half an hour everyone was talking of the tailor's meeting with the devil. There was such a throwing down of tools and clattering of tongues that the village priest put on his hat and walked out to find the cause of the hubbub. At first he listened with grave concern but when they came to the strange order which the devil had given to the tailor, he burst out laughing, and sent them all back to their work.

"Send the tailor to me before he begins work on the coat," he said, "and the rest of you, go on with your work as if nothing had happened."

The villagers went back to work, but the priest's strange behaviour set more tongues wagging; and when the tailor came out of the priest's study with a smile on his face they could scarcely contain themselves for curiosity. But the tailor would tell no-one what the pastor had said to him. He went quietly home and began the coat.

A week later, he stood in the dark lane again and at the very moment when he had first appeared, the devil jumped out of the earth and stood before him.

"Have you finished the coat?" he said in a threatening voice.

"I have," replied the tailor calmly. "Then on with it. Let's see if you can cut and stitch as well as you can talk".

The tailor unwrapped the coat and helped the devil into it, taking better care of his fingers this time. The devil pulled it round him, and then holding up the left sleeve, said in an angry voice, "This sleeve! Look at it, it is far too short!"

"Yes, I thought that might be so," replied the tailor, "so I made the other a little longer." The devil held up the sleeve, and finding it was so, and that he could not grumble at that on the score of length, looked round for other faults.

"What sort of pocket have you made here? I can't get my hand into it." "Never mind, I've made the other big enough. Look it's wide enough and deep enough to hold a brace of pheasants."

"And what about this tail? it's down to my ankles, you rogue!" "Is it? Then you will find the other is just your measure, for I've made it much shorter."

And so the argument continued. For everything the devil found wrong, the tailor showed him something right. If the stitching was loose here, it was tight there; if the buttons were too bright in one place, they were duller in another. There was no fault but the tailor could point out some perfection to counter-balance it, and in the end the devil seeing that he had been completely outwitted, flung down a handful of coins and disappeared. The tailor did not bother to pick them up. He walked home with greater sobriety and slept more soundly than for many a year.

Big Tom

The sun went down in a coppery west,
The grey sea called in its mad unrest;
The fishermen knew that husky roar,
So the boats were hauled far up the shore,
And the bearded giants loitered round,
Silent, and surly, and weatherbound.
Chilly and shrill the east wind blew,
And soon the quivering foam-flakes flew —
Flew like birds in the darkling air,
And dappled the moorland here and there;
The last rays gleamed on the Cheviot Hill,
And soon the cottages all were still.

Long by the glow of the dying fire
Big Tom sat still as the gale rose higher,
His mighty sons were all asleep;
Brooding he sat, and his thoughts were deep.
As the clamorous dark by the wind was torn,
He said, "There'll be death in the bay the morn."
Grimly rising, he shook his head,
The flooring quaked to his giant tread.

Once more he looked at the warring night,
And saw the fierce waves coiling white –
Coiling white in their aimless wrath,
Drenching with spray the village path,
Lightening through the troublous gloom,
Shaking the rocks with their sullen boom.
"Forty year on the coast," said he,
"But there never was such an ugly sea;
Some of the ships'll be running north,
Maybe they'll try to make the Forth;
They may try our Point, but they'll not get round,
They'll be nailed like rats in a trap, and drowned.
Reckon I'll not turn in just yet;
They said they'd waken me, may be forget."

So Tom sat on in his patient way
Till he saw the quiver of rising day.
And soon his sonorous voice rang high;
"Out, my lads, as quick as you can!
Out on the rocks here every man!
See here, there, away to the south,
Running, by God, to the Badger's Mouth!
At the westerly hollow they'll catch the squall, –
Lord, Have mercy upon them all!"

Every villager soon stood by,
Silently straining every eye;
For a labouring brig to the northward crept.
Our men looked grave, and the women wept –
Wept till many an eye was red,
For the little ship was sore beset.
How could she ever hope to ride
With the wreck of the foremast over her side?
She wallowed before the smashing seas;
Her scanty topsail caught the breeze,
But the deadly foremast dragged her sore,
And she settled and settled more and more.
She reeled and wavered with every shock:
Said Tom, "She'll drive on the Fairy Rock."
Lunging and straining, she neared our home,
Buried in wreaths of whirling foam;
We saw the signals were flying there,
When her mast heaved up in the misty air.
Signals! Alas! We all could tell,
She soon must sink in that boiling hell.

The farmers and folk from the market town
Had heard the gale, and they crowded down,
Their horses were tethered in restless troops,
The beach was dotted with curious groups;
And they stared to seaward, and held their breath
While the fated seamen wrestled with death.
Little by little the brig came on,
The Race engulfed her, her chance was gone;
She lurched, and a woman shrieked, "Oh, Lord!"
As the second mast went by the board.
Round and round in the desperate whirl,
Into the gap where the breakers swirl –
Smash! – and a quivering to and fro.
Said Tom, "They'll soon be with last year's snow."

Down to the beach the fishers rushed,
Right where the screaming back-draught gushed;
A sigh, and a lull of wind came then,
And they heard the cries of the dying men.
Then Mary Brown said, "Oh, Tom, my man,
Help them poor mortals if you can,
See, there's one of them waving there!
Hark! it's more than my heart can bear.
Tom, oh, man, we've lads of our own,
Would you like *them* to die alone?
Think of that poor bit bairn last year,
That came ashore to norrad of here;
He'd gripped a spar in his poor bit hand,
And his eyes were full of the cruel sand –
His bonny eyes, they stared – oh, me!–
The eyes his mother would never see;

100

She'd wait, and wait, and her heart would ache –
And I kissed the bairn for the mother's sake.
The ship has hardly an hour to stand,
And the corpses will come on the windy sand.
And it's oh! for the hearts so sad and sore,
For the lads that never go back no more.
If I lost you, Tom, I think I'd die,
But try to save them, my darling, try."

The giant patted her arm and smiled:
"Whisht, my bonny, thou's talking wild,
Give us a minute to look around,
And ask Big Harry to clear the ground,

Drive the loafers back to the wall,
And I'll see if there's any chance at all."

Then he sternly clenched his iron jaw,
Flashed a look, and a chance he saw –
For one grim instant he scanned the crowd,
Then like a trumpet his voice rang loud:
"Lay hold of the boat on the Dead Man's Ledge,
And haul her down to the water's edge."
A score of the bearded fellows ran
To do the hest of their foremost man.
Then he said, "My lads, it's a nasty sea,
But they mustn't drown – that cannot be.
I'm going to try and land them here, –
Which of you all will volunteer?"

Out stepped Harry, his eldest son;
"All right, father, I'll make one."
"Right my son; jump on to your throft;
I thowt that none o' the breed was soft!"
Then the second son, without a word,
Vaulted in, and a groan was heard,
And Mary muttered, "My three, my best!
Thy will be done! I will trust the rest."

Now, among the crowd who had come to stare
Was a carter driving a mettled mare.
She pawed, and foamed, and tried to rear,
For the yell of the wind sent her mad with fear.
Sudden she took the bit in her teeth,
And plunged from the road to the beach beneath;
"Hold her! stop her! catch at the rein,
Swing her round to the road again."
But the creature was furious, fierce and fleet,
She spurned the sand with her flying feet;
Out of the cart the man was hurled,
Over his head the wheels were whirled,
And the mare rushed on, with her lightning dash,

Right on the coble. There came a crash –
A tearing struggle. The crowd looked blank,
For the axle had torn clean through a plank.
Poor Tom bent down, and his brow grew dark,
For the gap was below the water mark.

And the only boat with a chance to live
Was about as safe as a miller's sieve.
But, glory of glories, this hero then
Waved his hand to calm the men,
Quietly took off his shaggy coat,
Lightly vaulted into the boat,
And before a soul had time to speak
He stuffed his jacket into the leak.
Then he roared, "I want another lad;
Come away hinnies – it's not so bad;
One of you hold this in and bale
And I'll bet my lugs we shall not fail."
His third son cheerfully stepped on board,
And Mary murmered, "Oh! mercy, Lord!"

So we shoved them off in the weltering bay,
And the straining giants rowed away.
Up like a bird on the roller's crown,
Poising a little, then swiftly down.
Ah! that's over her! Steady! No!
Like a wild sea-bird then see her go.
Squelch! and a comber lightly rolls
Over the bow – Lord help their souls!
Here a monster comes charging on,
Starboard! a lurch, and the wave is gone.

Yard by yard they fight their way,
"Harry is done for!" "What did you say?"
Didn't you see him drop his oar,
Making as if he could pull no more?
Never a bit, just watch him strike,
Tearing hard – saw you ever the like?
Yard by yard they lash their way
Through the curtain of driving spray.
"Over she goes." "I see her keel."
"Lord's sake, what does their mother feel?"
"Elsies's a stagger!" "He's baling hard."
Still she bangs at it yard by yard –
Yard by yard she's drawing near;
"Off with your hats, boys, give them a cheer!
Three times three, and just one more."

Look at the gallant fellows now,
See them rolling under her bow,
One has jumped, two, three, four, five, –
Lord, pray fetch them back alive –

Six they've got, and her nose is round;
Steady, my lads, you're homeward bound!
There's a thunderer bowled them on,
"Oh! my sons, they all are gone!"
Mary screamed, and rushed from the track,
Tried for the sea, but they held her back.
The foam cleared off, then came a lull,
And we saw the tortured boat half full,
Settling steadily by the head.
Mary bit her lip till it bled,
But the dauntless fellows had not failed;
Madly the rescued sailors baled –
Baled with sou'westers and clumsy bowls.
See, she's lighter! Watch how she rolls!
One stroke more – it isn't far!
Round with her starn now – here we are!
Then with a wild and joyous din
We plunge through the foam, and haul them in.

A laugh like that of a joyous child,
Shrills through the air – poor Mary's wild.
"Oh! my bonny, the Lord is good!
My heart was breaking as I stood;
But I knew He would fetch you back again,
For Hisself He gave His life for men."
And Harry, the shaggy eldest lad,
Grinned, and said, "We've not done bad."

Then we cheered them home to the cottage door,
And we put the boat in safe once more;
And every soul of our rugged race
Was proud that the men belonged our place.
They had never a sign of praise or pay,
They wanted none – it was not their way.
But I've tried to tell with my clumsy pen
The bravest deed of the sons of men.

James Runciman.

■ Enigma: The machine from U-110.

■ Action stations: War-time picture of Captain Joe Baker-Cresswell.

Captain Baker-Cresswell, D.S.O., RN, died on March 4th 1997 and his wife Rona a month later. Details of his life are on page 5.

The most significant event in his career was the capture of the German submarine U110.

He was on the point of ramming it, but a last minute decision decided that its capture was possible.

This decision resulted in the retrieval of the Enigma coding machine, thus enabling the code breakers of Bletchley Park to break the code. Thus, the movements of German U-boats were known, resulting in the saving of many cargo ships and lives.

King George VI on investing Capt. Baker-Cresswell with the D.S.O. said that it was one of the most important events of the war. Winston Churchill also added his praise.

The recent TV programme, 'Station X', gave details of the importance of the capture.